To Natalie
Christmas 2006
Grandma & Grandpa Stein

Eyewitness
MUSIC

Tambourine

Triangle

19th-century Finnish *kantele*

Indian transverse flute

Four-keyed English flute, c. 1811

Moroccan lute with feather plectrum

17th-century German kit

19th-century German *ocarina* (vessel flute)

Pellet drum

19th-century Chinese *sihu* (spike fiddle) and bow

Tuba
mouthpiece

Horn and trumpet
mouthpieces

Eyewitness
MUSIC

Written by
NEIL ARDLEY

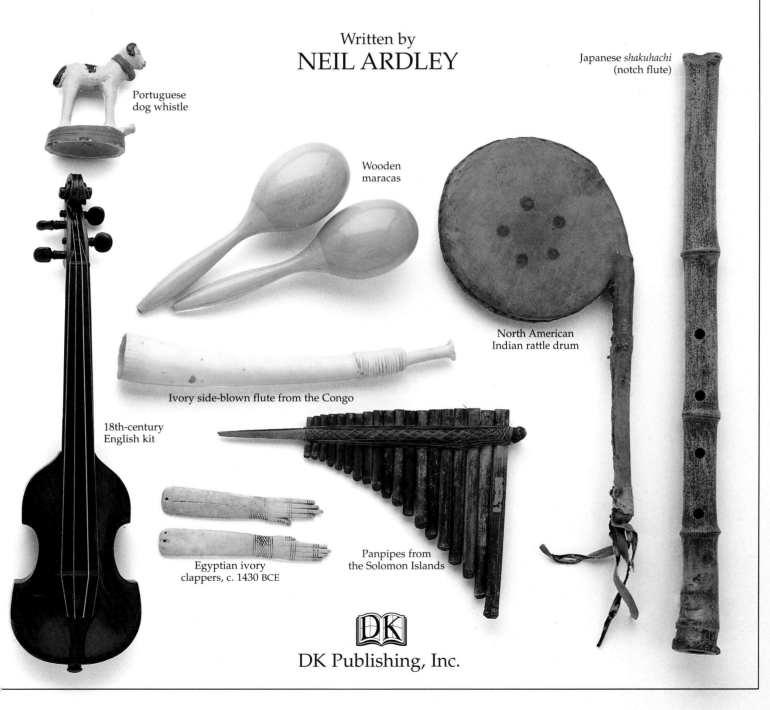

Japanese *shakuhachi*
(notch flute)

Portuguese
dog whistle

Wooden
maracas

North American
Indian rattle drum

Ivory side-blown flute from the Congo

18th-century
English kit

Egyptian ivory
clappers, c. 1430 BCE

Panpipes from
the Solomon Islands

DK

DK Publishing, Inc.

Double reeds

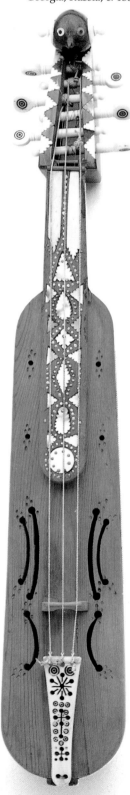

Black Sea fiddle, from Georgia, Russia, c. 1865

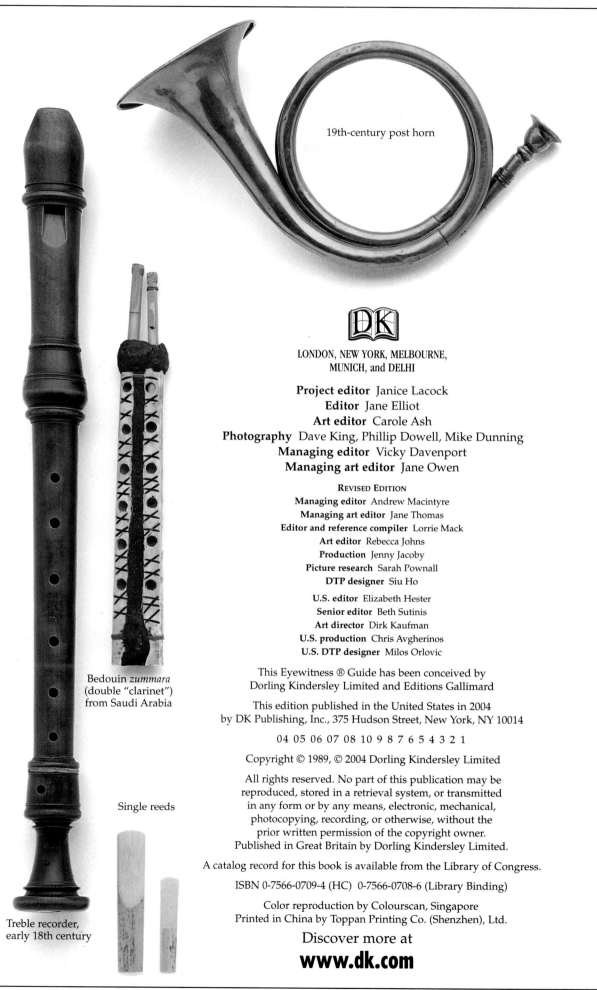

19th-century post horn

Bedouin *zummara*
(double "clarinet")
from Saudi Arabia

Single reeds

Treble recorder,
early 18th century

DK

LONDON, NEW YORK, MELBOURNE, MUNICH, and DELHI

Project editor Janice Lacock
Editor Jane Elliot
Art editor Carole Ash
Photography Dave King, Phillip Dowell, Mike Dunning
Managing editor Vicky Davenport
Managing art editor Jane Owen

REVISED EDITION
Managing editor Andrew Macintyre
Managing art editor Jane Thomas
Editor and reference compiler Lorrie Mack
Art editor Rebecca Johns
Production Jenny Jacoby
Picture research Sarah Pownall
DTP designer Siu Ho

U.S. editor Elizabeth Hester
Senior editor Beth Sutinis
Art director Dirk Kaufman
U.S. production Chris Avgherinos
U.S. DTP designer Milos Orlovic

This Eyewitness ® Guide has been conceived by
Dorling Kindersley Limited and Editions Gallimard

This edition published in the United States in 2004
by DK Publishing, Inc., 375 Hudson Street, New York, NY 10014

04 05 06 07 08 10 9 8 7 6 5 4 3 2 1

Copyright © 1989, © 2004 Dorling Kindersley Limited

A catalog record for this book is available from the Library of Congress.

ISBN 0-7566-0709-4 (HC) 0-7566-0708-6 (Library Binding)

Color reproduction by Colourscan, Singapore
Printed in China by Toppan Printing Co. (Shenzhen), Ltd.

Discover more at
www.dk.com

Contents

Castanets

18th-century
French flageolet

Seeing sound

THE WORLD OF MUSIC is a kaleidoscope of sound. With most instruments it is easy to see how the different types of sound are made. Blowing a flute obviously gives a totally different sound from banging a drum. But you do not have to watch people playing to tell a flute from a drum or any other instrument - you can recognize the sounds. Playing an instrument makes part of it vibrate rapidly back and forth. The vibration produces sound waves in the air, which travel to our ears. The waves are small, but they cause rapid changes in air pressure at the same rate as the vibration of the instrument. The sound wave from each instrument makes its own kind of pressure changes. These can be shown by curved and jagged lines that are called waveforms (right). Each waveform is created by a particular pattern of vibration in an instrument. The sound of music causes our eardrums to vibrate in the same pattern as the instrument being played. These vibrations are "translated" by the brain so that we can recognize which instrument is being played.

Medieval musicians shown outside a cathedral in a Flemish prayer book

TUNING FORK
A tuning fork makes a very pure sound. The prongs vibrate regularly, creating a sound with a curving waveform. The rate at which the peaks pass gives the pitch. Faster vibrations produce a higher note.

VIOLIN
The violin makes a bright sound that has a jagged waveform. The violin sound shown here has the same pitch as the tuning fork. As a result the peaks of the waves produced by the violin are the same distance apart, and pass at the same rate, as those produced by the tuning fork.

FLUTE
The flute is playing the same note as the tuning fork and violin. The waveform of its sound is more curved than jagged, because the flute produces a purer, more mellow sound than the violin, with only a touch of brightness. In spite of this difference, the peaks of the waveform are the same distance apart and pass at the same rate.

GONG
Hitting a gong or a cymbal makes it vibrate in an irregular pattern. The crashing sound has a jagged, random waveform. We hear such waveforms as a noise with little or no recognizable pitch.

COMBINED WAVES
When people play together, the sound waves from their instruments combine. Our ears receive the combined sound waves, making the eardrums vibrate with a very complex sound pattern. Yet our brains are able to sort out the different instruments playing.

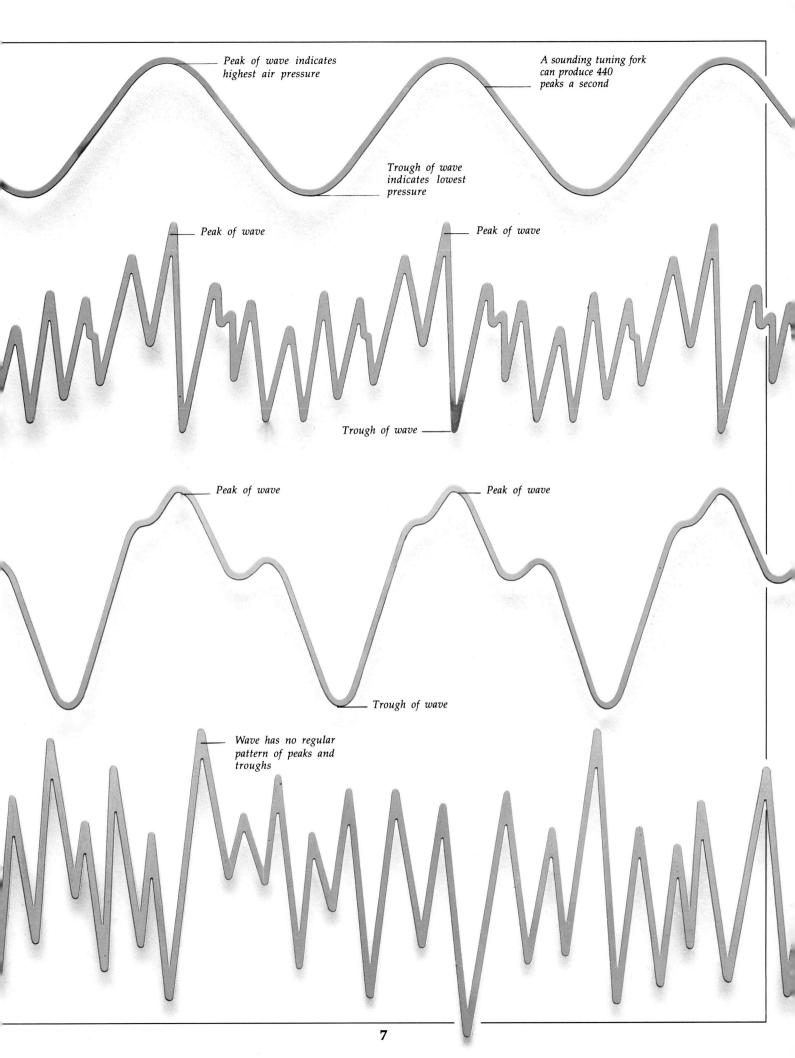

Peak of wave indicates highest air pressure

A sounding tuning fork can produce 440 peaks a second

Trough of wave indicates lowest pressure

Peak of wave

Peak of wave

Trough of wave

Peak of wave

Peak of wave

Trough of wave

Wave has no regular pattern of peaks and troughs

Wind tunnels

"AN ILL WIND THAT BLOWS NO GOOD," to paraphrase a well-known proverb, might well sum up wind instruments: a poorly played saxophone, for example, can sound like a cow in distress, but in trained hands (and mouth) it can create a rich diversity of sounds. There are two main families of wind instruments: woodwind and brass. Basically all brass instruments were once made of metal, while all woodwind instruments were once made of wood – hence their names. The categories have stuck regardless of what they are made of today. Both kinds of instruments are essentially a hollow tube with a mouthpiece. Blowing into the mouthpiece makes the air inside the tube vibrate. The length of vibrating air is called the air column. Making it shorter raises the pitch, and the notes sound higher. Brass instruments, like the trumpet, have another way of raising the pitch. Blowing harder into the mouthpiece makes the air column split, so that it vibrates in two halves, three thirds and so on, to give higher notes.

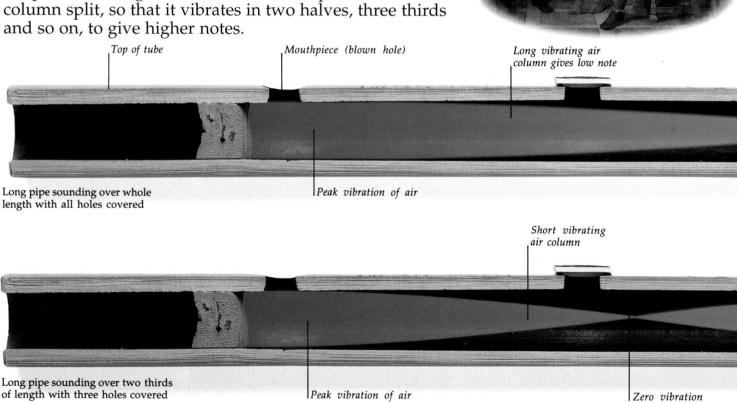

Top of tube

Mouthpiece (blown hole)

Long vibrating air column gives low note

Peak vibration of air

Long pipe sounding over whole length with all holes covered

Short vibrating air column

Long pipe sounding over two thirds of length with three holes covered

Peak vibration of air

Zero vibration

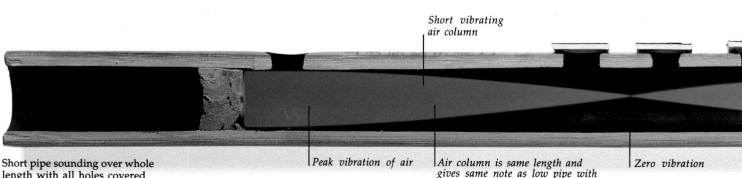

Short vibrating air column

Short pipe sounding over whole length with all holes covered

Peak vibration of air

Air column is same length and gives same note as low pipe with three holes covered

Zero vibration

Multi-shaped mouthpieces

Modern brass instruments use metal mouthpieces in the shape of a cup or funnel pressed against the player's lips (and none of them use reeds). The shape of these mouthpieces affects the sound: deep funnel-shapes, as on a horn, produce a smooth tone, while cup-shaped mouthpieces, as on a trumpet, result in greater sharpness. Woodwinds either use reeds or have mouthpieces into or over which the player blows.

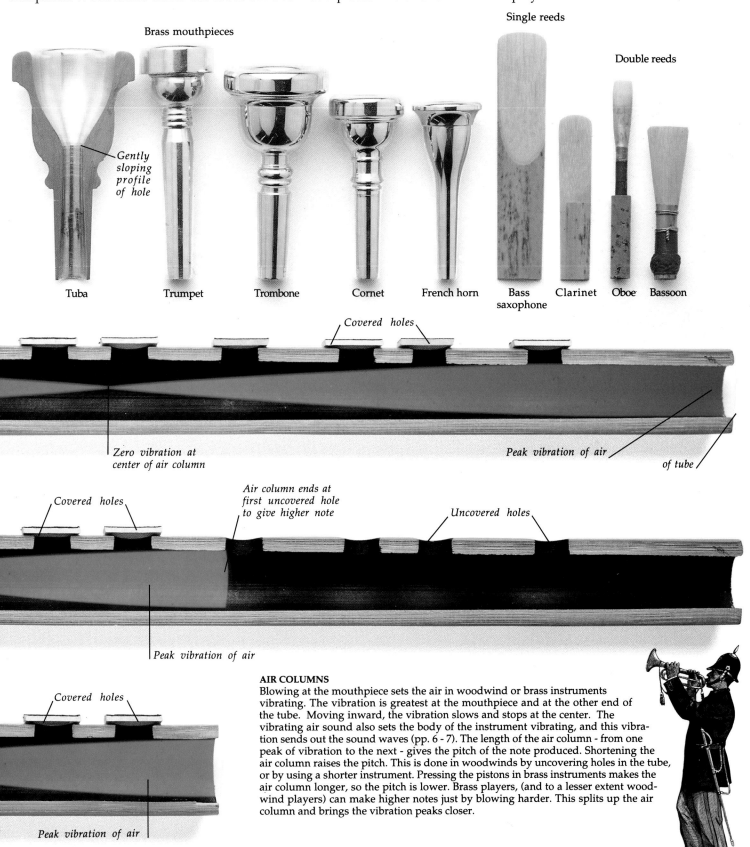

Brass mouthpieces

Single reeds

Double reeds

Gently sloping profile of hole

Tuba   Trumpet   Trombone   Cornet   French horn   Bass saxophone   Clarinet   Oboe   Bassoon

Covered holes

Zero vibration at center of air column

Peak vibration of air

of tube

Covered holes

Air column ends at first uncovered hole to give higher note

Uncovered holes

Peak vibration of air

Covered holes

Peak vibration of air

AIR COLUMNS

Blowing at the mouthpiece sets the air in woodwind or brass instruments vibrating. The vibration is greatest at the mouthpiece and at the other end of the tube. Moving inward, the vibration slows and stops at the center. The vibrating air sound also sets the body of the instrument vibrating, and this vibration sends out the sound waves (pp. 6 - 7). The length of the air column - from one peak of vibration to the next - gives the pitch of the note produced. Shortening the air column raises the pitch. This is done in woodwinds by uncovering holes in the tube, or by using a shorter instrument. Pressing the pistons in brass instruments makes the air column longer, so the pitch is lower. Brass players, (and to a lesser extent woodwind players) can make higher notes just by blowing harder. This splits up the air column and brings the vibration peaks closer.

The Pied Piper lured children from Hamelin

Pipes and flutes

THE BREATHY, INTIMATE SOUND of pipes and flutes gives them a haunting quality. Perhaps this is why they have long been associated with magic - as in Mozart's opera *The Magic Flute*, and the legend of the Pied Piper of Hamelin, whose music enchanted the children from the town. Sound is made simply by blowing across the end of an open pipe or a hole in the pipe (p. 8). This sets the air inside the pipe vibrating to give a lovely, mellow tone, to which the air escaping around the hole adds a distinctive hiss. Blowing harder into the pipe produces higher notes.

Notch

WHISTLING FISH
Although it looks totally unlike a recorder, this pottery fish makes music in a similar way. Both have ducts - short channels that lead air from the mouth to a blowhole in the side.

SEEING DOUBLE
Flageolets, a group of wind instruments that taper away from the mouthpiece end, are often played in folk music. The tin whistle is an example. This intricately carved wooden instrument from Yugoslavia is a double flageolet with two pipes that can be played separately. It dates from about 1900, but the instrument has been known since the 1200s.

Blowholes

Notch

Finger holes

EARLY MUSIC
Whistles made of reindeer toe bones date from 40,000 B.C. These French bones may have been used for signaling rather than to make music.

MUSIC FROM FRUIT
This whistle from the Sudan (North Africa) is made from a piece of gourd. It is played by blowing into a notch in the open end and closing the holes with fingers.

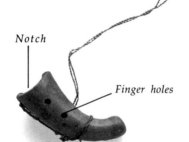

Double set of finger holes

Each pipe played by a different hand

Blowhole

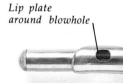

Lip plate around blowhole

STONE ANIMALS
The frogs and eagle are unusual and attractive decorations on this 19th-century flageolet. It was carved in soapstone by the Haida Indians, a tribe who live on islands off Canada.

MUSIC OF THE GODS
Panpipes get their name from the myth of the Greek god Pan. When the nymph that Pan loved was turned into a reed, he cut the reed into a set of different length pipes, which he played to console himself. Today panpipes are most often associated with South American music.

ORIENTAL DESIGN
The notch cut in the end of the Japanese *shakuhachi* might make it easier to play than simple end-blown flutes such as panpipes.

Elaborately carved wood in the shape of a dragon's head

Transverse flutes

Any pipe with finger holes and a blown end or hole can be called a flute, but the name is usually given only to instruments that sound by being blown across a hole. These are classified as transverse, or side-blown, flutes and are held horizontally.

HANDY DEVICE
Although blown like a transverse flute, this bamboo instrument from Guyana (South America) is unusual in that the player changes the note by blocking and changing the shape of the large opening in the side with one hand.

Opening covered by the hand to change the note

Blowhole

Blowhole

Some pipes and flutes can be blown with the nose as well as the mouth

NOSE NOISE
Nose flutes are very common in the Pacific area. This beautifully decorated bamboo example comes from Fiji. It has a blowhole at each end and three finger holes in the center. The player blows with one nostril, blocking the other with his hand - or with tobacco!

THE BOEHM SYSTEM
The flute was greatly improved by the German instrument-maker Theobald Boehm (1794-1881), who invented a key system in which pads, operated by keys or the fingers, covered all the holes. This gave a better sound and made the flute easier to play.

HIGH NOTES
The piccolo is a small, high-pitched flute invented in the late 1700s. This early wooden example has a single key. The modern instrument can be played by flautists because it has the same type of keys (keywork) as the concert flute.

Finger holes

Keys

Early wooden flute, c. 1830

Thumb keys

Keys for little fingers

Modern concert flute

FROM SIMPLICITY TO SOPHISTICATION
The concert flute, with its superior sound, passed the recorder and flageolet in popularity during the 1800s. The simple keywork of the early wooden instrument contrasts with the complex keywork of the modern metal flute, but the modern instrument is easier to play and has a brighter sound.

Pad closed by finger

Pad closed by key

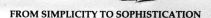

DRAGON FLUTE
The *lung ti*, or dragon flute, is an elegant and unusual Chinese transverse flute used in religious ceremonies. It is made of lacquered bamboo and has a thin sheet of paper covering the blowhole. This gives it a penetrating, buzzing sound.

Ornate lacquer decoration

Vibrating reeds

This detail from a 17th-century painting shows two shawm players, accompanied by a trombonist, taking part in a festival procession in Spain

TO MAKE A HOLLOW CANE into a musical instrument, just cut a short length, flatten or slice through one end, and bore a few holes. Although it will produce little more than a squawk, this primitive pipe is the ancestor of all reed instruments. The distinctive, reedy sound is caused by a vibrating slice of cane called a beating reed. The result is a variety of sounds that range from the liquid notes of the clarinet to the wistful tones of the oboe and the gruff blurts of the bassoon.

Single reeds

Clarinets and saxophones (p. 14) are played with a mouthpiece containing a metal ligature (band) that holds in place a single reed. The player's mouth can influence the vibration of the reed to produce individual tones.

The soprano clarinet is the most played member of the clarinet family. This one is made of African blackwood

Deep-sounding clarinets like this alto clarinet have a curved tube

Clarinet reed

Mouthpiece

Barrel joint can be moved to adjust tuning

Head joint with keys for left hand

The normal position for a clarinet to be played

Keys for right little finger

Keys for left little finger

Middle joint with keys for right hand

Key for left thumb

Holder for music stand

Ring for neck sling

Cork ring to seal joints

The tube of a clarinet widens only at the bell

Keys for right index finger

Extra key to extend range

SHRILL BUT SWEET
Clarinets were developed during the 18th century, and the awkward keys were improved by Boehm (p. 11) about a century later. The name was inspired by the fact that the high notes suggested the sound of a trumpet or *clarino*. The sound, somewhat shrill and sweet, is widely used in orchestral music. A more lively, even wild, approach to playing the clarinet can be heard in traditional jazz and some folk music.

Metal bell projects sound forward

Right-hand rest

Keys for right thumb (finger holes on other side)

Metal cap over bend in wooden tube

Bulb-shaped bell gives the cor anglais its soft, velvety sound.

Double reds

Two slices of cane make up the double reed, which vibrates to sound the column of air in the tube of the instrument. The double reed and cone-shaped tube give the piercing, somewhat nasal sound of the oboe, cor anglais, and bassoon.

A neck sling is used to support the weight of the bassoon

Most German bassoons have a decorative ivory ring around the bell

For ease of playing, the double reed fits into a curved tube called a crook

MAKING A DOUBLE REED
A strip of cane is cut and bent in two (1). The ends are bound together and fitted into a cork-covered tube called a staple, and the bend is sliced off (2). Finally, the tops of the reeds are scraped (3).

1   2   3

Staple

DEEP BREATH
The thin opening of a double reed restricts the air flow, which means a long phrase (group of notes) can be played in one breath.

"A SEA GOD SPEAKING"
Impressed by its deep, dark tones, Sacheverell Sitwell, the writer, thus described the sound of the bassoon. It is mainly an orchestral instrument. A wooden tube, measuring 9 ft (2.7 m), doubles back on itself within the body of the instrument. Unlike other woodwind instruments, the bassoon has not undergone key improvements and is awkward to play.

Double reed in short bent crook

The bent crook also helps the player to hold the cor anglais, or English horn, at a comfortable angle for the hands

Keys for left thumb (finger holes on other side)

The keys of the cor anglais are exactly the same as the oboe, but without the oboe's lowest notes

A SAD MYSTERY
The cor anglais is a low-pitched oboe with a soft, sad sound. The instrument was originally curved like a hunting horn, and in the 19th century the curve hardened into an angle. Its name is a partial mystery. *Cor anglais* is French for "English horn," and it is often called by this name, but while the velvety tone of the cor anglais recalls the sound of a distant horn, no one is sure why it is called "English."

Double reed fits into the head of the oboe

CHARMED NOTES
The snake charmer's *tiktiri*, a double clarinet, is made of two cane pipes in a gourd.

Low key missing from the cor anglais

Musician playing a modern oboe

HIGH WOOD
The oboe is descended from the shawm, a simple pipe with a double reed played in folk music. Its name derives from *hautbois*, the French name for the shawm, which means "high wood." The oboe is known for its high, sad tones, but it can be harsh in the low register.

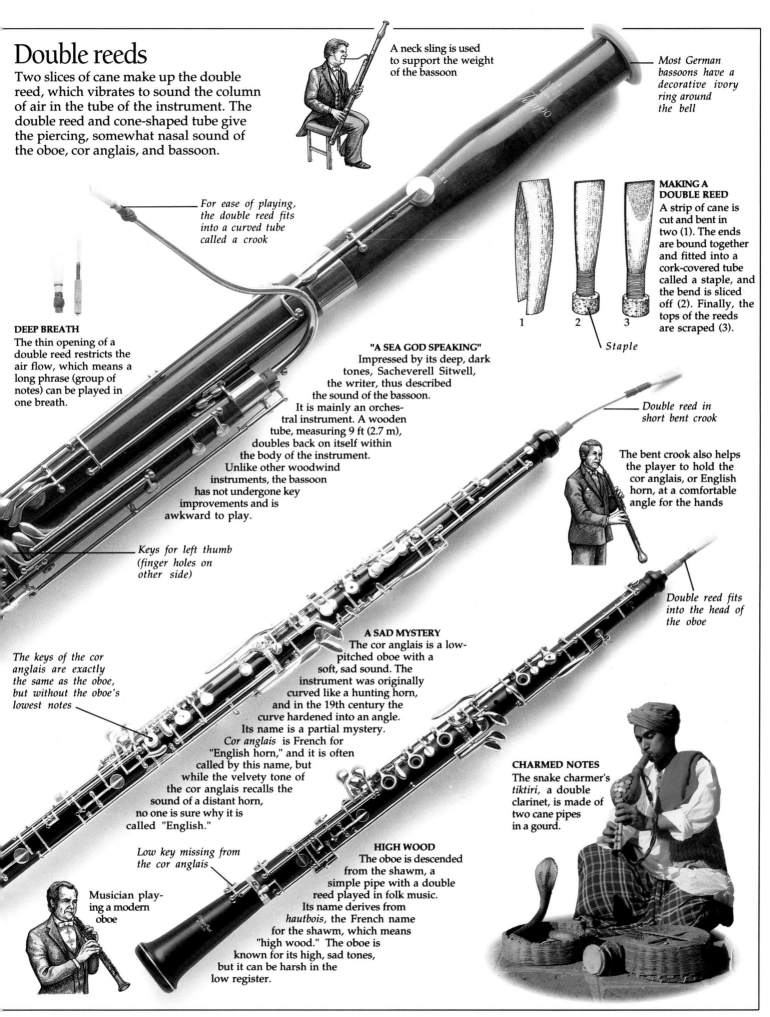

Long-lasting hybrids

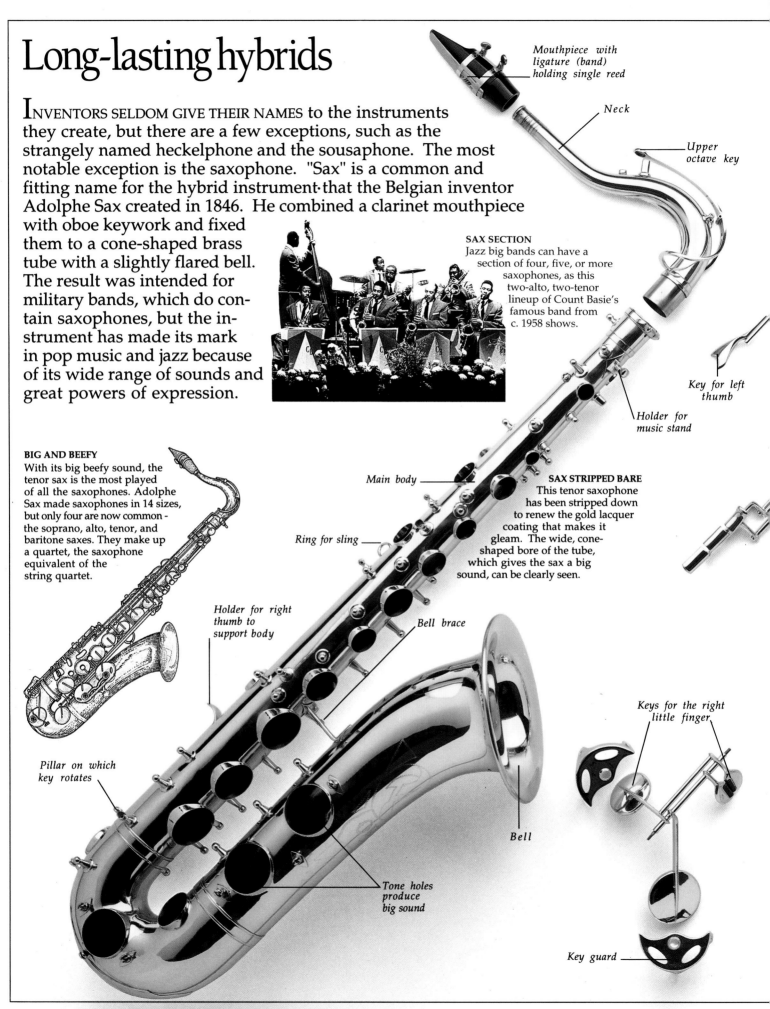

INVENTORS SELDOM GIVE THEIR NAMES to the instruments they create, but there are a few exceptions, such as the strangely named heckelphone and the sousaphone. The most notable exception is the saxophone. "Sax" is a common and fitting name for the hybrid instrument that the Belgian inventor Adolphe Sax created in 1846. He combined a clarinet mouthpiece with oboe keywork and fixed them to a cone-shaped brass tube with a slightly flared bell. The result was intended for military bands, which do contain saxophones, but the instrument has made its mark in pop music and jazz because of its wide range of sounds and great powers of expression.

Mouthpiece with ligature (band) holding single reed

Neck

Upper octave key

SAX SECTION
Jazz big bands can have a section of four, five, or more saxophones, as this two-alto, two-tenor lineup of Count Basie's famous band from c. 1958 shows.

Key for left thumb

Holder for music stand

BIG AND BEEFY
With its big beefy sound, the tenor sax is the most played of all the saxophones. Adolphe Sax made saxophones in 14 sizes, but only four are now common – the soprano, alto, tenor, and baritone saxes. They make up a quartet, the saxophone equivalent of the string quartet.

Main body

SAX STRIPPED BARE
This tenor saxophone has been stripped down to renew the gold lacquer coating that makes it gleam. The wide, cone-shaped bore of the tube, which gives the sax a big sound, can be clearly seen.

Ring for sling

Holder for right thumb to support body

Bell brace

Pillar on which key rotates

Keys for the right little finger

Bell

Tone holes produce big sound

Key guard

14

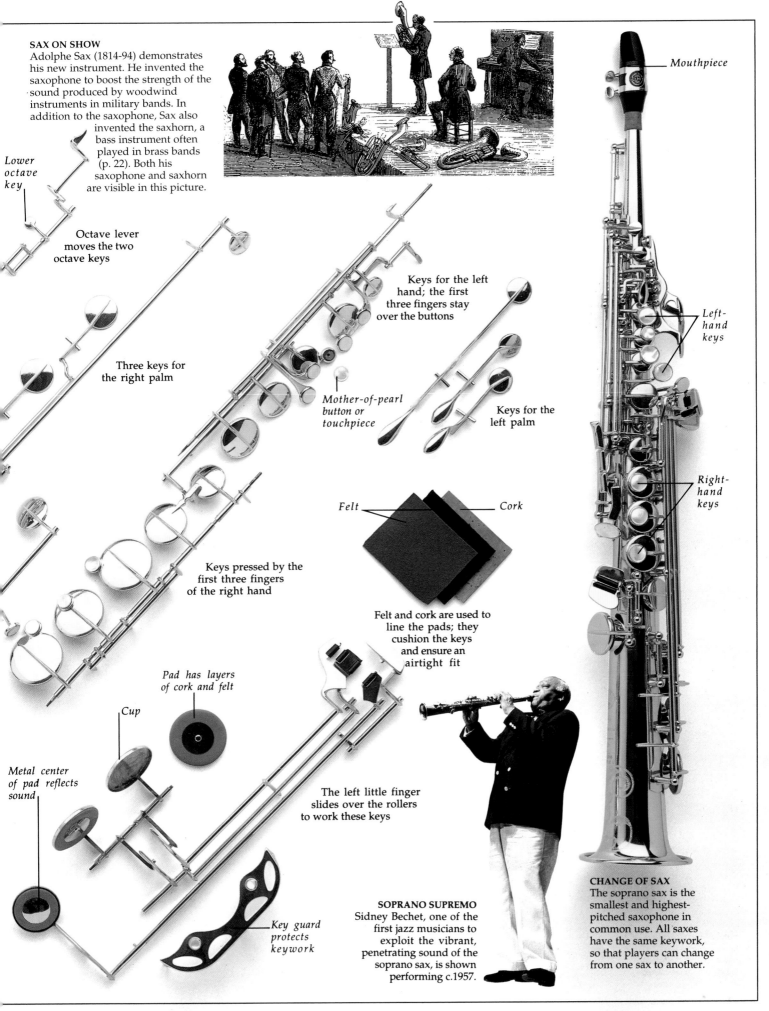

SAX ON SHOW
Adolphe Sax (1814-94) demonstrates his new instrument. He invented the saxophone to boost the strength of the sound produced by woodwind instruments in military bands. In addition to the saxophone, Sax also invented the saxhorn, a bass instrument often played in brass bands (p. 22). Both his saxophone and saxhorn are visible in this picture.

Lower octave key

Octave lever moves the two octave keys

Keys for the left hand; the first three fingers stay over the buttons

Three keys for the right palm

Mother-of-pearl button or touchpiece

Keys for the left palm

Felt   *Cork*

Keys pressed by the first three fingers of the right hand

Felt and cork are used to line the pads; they cushion the keys and ensure an airtight fit

Mouthpiece

Left-hand keys

Right-hand keys

Pad has layers of cork and felt

Cup

Metal center of pad reflects sound

The left little finger slides over the rollers to work these keys

Key guard protects keywork

SOPRANO SUPREMO
Sidney Bechet, one of the first jazz musicians to exploit the vibrant, penetrating sound of the soprano sax, is shown performing c.1957.

CHANGE OF SAX
The soprano sax is the smallest and highest-pitched saxophone in common use. All saxes have the same keywork, so that players can change from one sax to another.

Bags of sound

TAKING A BREATH is a problem that faces all wind players. A few overcome it by the amazing feat of breathing in through the nose and blowing out through the mouth at the same time. A more common solution is to separate the reed from the mouth and activate the reed by squeezing a bag filled with air held under one arm, as in the bagpipes. Accordions and harmonicas have free reeds; when blown by an air stream, these reeds vibrate to give a note without having a pipe. The result, in the case of bagpipes, is a strident, rough sound, which is called a skirl.

Traditional 19th-century Scottish bagpiper

A carved wooden goat's head is a traditional feature of central European bagpipes

Drone

A BELLOWING GOAT
This ornately carved bellows-blown bagpipe was made in Hungary in the early 20th century. The bellows are placed under the arm and pumped in and out to blow up the goatskin bag. The curved pipe contains a reed and sounds one continuous low note in the drone. The bag also blows a pair of reeds in the double chanter, which has fingerholes for both hands to play the melodies.

Air from the mouth of the goat's head blows the double chanter

The drone has a single beating reed and ends in a wide bell

The mouth pipe has a valve to keep air from leaving the bag

Kidskin bag

Bellows with straps to go around one arm

OLD WINDBAG
The *biniou* is a simple sheepskin bagpipe from Brittany in France. This instrument dates from the mid-19th century. The *biniou* is still played, often with a *bombard*, a type of shawm (p. 12), in performances of folk music. The piper blows into the mouth pipe to inflate the bag, which is then squeezed to sound the drone and chanter. Mouth-blown bagpipes of this kind are found throughout Europe, Africa, and Asia. The sound of Scottish pipes, which have three drone pipes, is very well known.

PEOPLE AT PLAY
A bagpipe features in this 16th-century painting by Breughel, who often portrayed people noisily enjoying themselves.

The single chanter is sounded by a double reed and has seven finger holes

The bag is made of sheepskin

Pushing the knob opens the lower row of holes to sound extra notes

Four of the 17 pipes are dummy pipes to balance the sheng

Band to hold the pipes together

FORM OF THE PHOENIX
The *sheng*, seen complete (far left) and in pieces (left and below), is a mouth organ that can be traced back 3,000 years to China. Its elegant shape is said to resemble the legendary bird the phoenix. The *sheng* is played by blowing into, and sucking air from, the wind chamber while fingering the holes in the pipes. Opening the holes admits air to the free reeds at the base of the bamboo pipes. The reeds are brass tongues that are weighted with wax to tune them.

A skilled Chinese musician playing a complicated mouth organ

SUCK AND BLOW
The mouth organ, or harmonica, has two sets of free reeds that sound as the player blows and sucks through the instrument. Derived from Asian mouth organs, the harmonica dates back only to the last century.

Finger holes

Wind chamber

Mouthpiece

Brass tongues

Lacquered wind chamber with holes for pipes

Keys made of ivory and blue plastic

Bellows blow and suck air through the reeds

A 19th-century busker (street musician) with his monkey and accordion

SQUEEZE AND WHEEZE
Floral bellows, a nickel-plated grate, and blue plastic fittings add to the splendor of the accordion. While accordions are often associated with France, this 20th-century instrument was made in Italy. Pressing the keys and buttons admits air from the bellows to sets of free metal reeds. The accordion is supported by straps, leaving the hands free to operate the bellows and play the keys and buttons.

The wheezy sound of the reeds emerges from the grate

120 buttons give bass notes and chords

Piped music

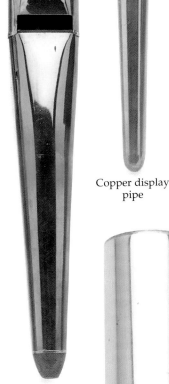

THOUSANDS OF PIPES may send echoes through a great cathedral as the organ plays, yet the ancestor of the mighty pipe organ is the humble panpipe (p. 10). Pressing the organ keys sends air to a series of pipes that sound in the same way as woodwind pipes (pp. 8-9). The first organ, invented in Greece in c. 250 B.C., cleverly used water power to blow the air through the pipes. Today electric fans do the job.

PORTABLE PIPES
The 15th-century portative organ could be carried around. One hand worked bellows to blow the air into a set of flue pipes. The other hand played the oddly-angled keys.

Copper display pipe

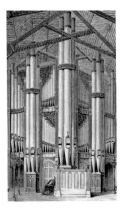

JUMBO PIPES
The lowest notes on a large organ may come from pipes almost 32 ft (10 m) long.

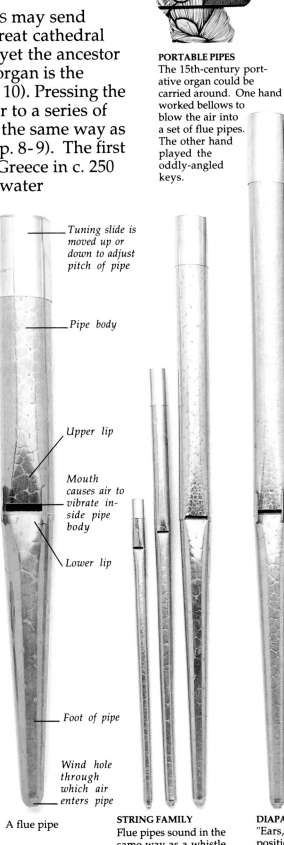

Tuning slide is moved up or down to adjust pitch of pipe

Pipe body

Upper lip

Mouth causes air to vibrate inside pipe body

Lower lip

Foot of pipe

Wind hole through which air enters pipe

A flue pipe

50% lead
50% tin

70% lead
30% tin

MIX OF METALS
Alloys of lead and tin are often used for organ pipes. Tin brightens the sound; lead dulls it.

STRING FAMILY
Flue pipes sound in the same way as a whistle (p. 10). These narrow pipes belong to the string family of organ pipes.

DIAPASON (BASIC) PIPES
"Ears," tiny metal flaps positioned each side of the "mouths" of the flue pipes, stabilize the sounds produced by the pipes.

DISPLAY PRINCIPAL
These pipes are so-called because they are on view in the front of the organ. They are made of 80% tin, giving a bright tone.

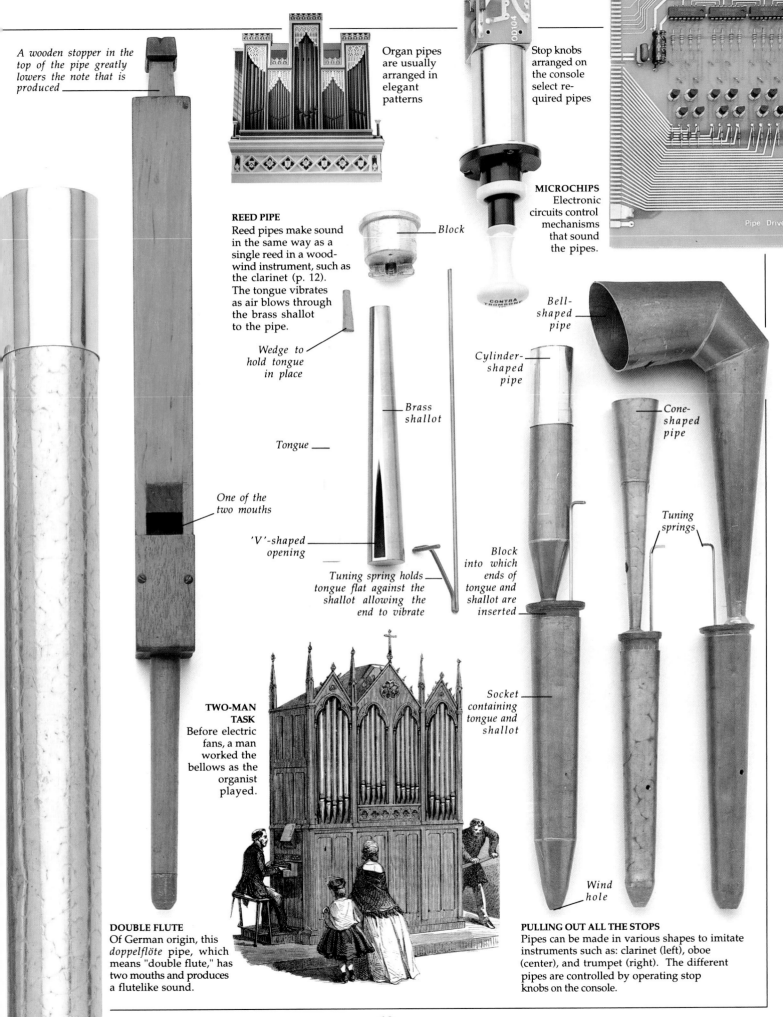

A wooden stopper in the top of the pipe greatly lowers the note that is produced

Organ pipes are usually arranged in elegant patterns

Stop knobs arranged on the console select required pipes

MICROCHIPS
Electronic circuits control mechanisms that sound the pipes.

REED PIPE
Reed pipes make sound in the same way as a single reed in a woodwind instrument, such as the clarinet (p. 12). The tongue vibrates as air blows through the brass shallot to the pipe.

Block

Wedge to hold tongue in place

Brass shallot

Tongue

One of the two mouths

'V'-shaped opening

Tuning spring holds tongue flat against the shallot allowing the end to vibrate

Block into which ends of tongue and shallot are inserted

Bell-shaped pipe

Cylinder-shaped pipe

Cone-shaped pipe

Tuning springs

Socket containing tongue and shallot

Wind hole

TWO-MAN TASK
Before electric fans, a man worked the bellows as the organist played.

DOUBLE FLUTE
Of German origin, this *doppelflöte* pipe, which means "double flute," has two mouths and produces a flutelike sound.

PULLING OUT ALL THE STOPS
Pipes can be made in various shapes to imitate instruments such as: clarinet (left), oboe (center), and trumpet (right). The different pipes are controlled by operating stop knobs on the console.

The cornu was a Roman horn made of bronze

Beginning of brass

German musicians of 1520: the two on the left are playing shawms (p. 12) and the one on the right a trumpet

As THEIR NAME SUGGESTS, the principal brass instruments, such as the trumpet, trombone, horn, and tuba, really are made of brass, usually lacquered or silver-plated for ease of cleaning. They have their origin, however, in natural instruments such as conch shells, hollowed branches, and animal horns. Brass tubes that can be sounded by the lips are ideal for fanfares and hunting calls, but they can sound only a limited number of notes. In the attempt to extend their musical range, inventors came up with some bizarre contrivances, including the aptly named serpent (p. 21)

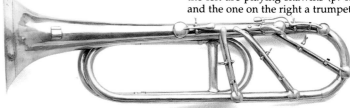

NOT THE KEY TO SUCCESS
Franz Joseph Haydn composed his famous trumpet concerto of 1796 for the newly designed keyed trumpet because it could produce extra notes. However, the instrument was said to sound like a "demented oboe" so it did not long survive.

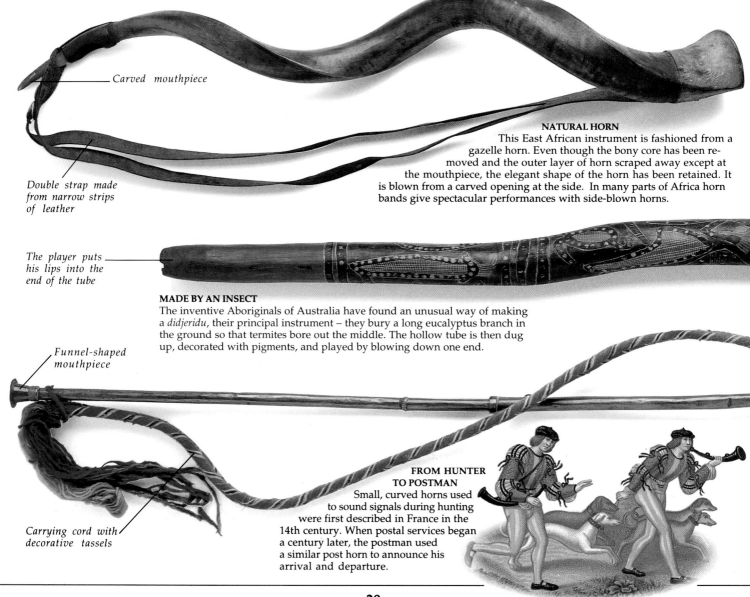

Carved mouthpiece

Double strap made from narrow strips of leather

NATURAL HORN
This East African instrument is fashioned from a gazelle horn. Even though the bony core has been removed and the outer layer of horn scraped away except at the mouthpiece, the elegant shape of the horn has been retained. It is blown from a carved opening at the side. In many parts of Africa horn bands give spectacular performances with side-blown horns.

The player puts his lips into the end of the tube

MADE BY AN INSECT
The inventive Aboriginals of Australia have found an unusual way of making a *didjeridu*, their principal instrument – they bury a long eucalyptus branch in the ground so that termites bore out the middle. The hollow tube is then dug up, decorated with pigments, and played by blowing down one end.

Funnel-shaped mouthpiece

FROM HUNTER TO POSTMAN
Small, curved horns used to sound signals during hunting were first described in France in the 14th century. When postal services began a century later, the postman used a similar post horn to announce his arrival and departure.

Carrying cord with decorative tassels

Detachable crook to lengthen the tube, thereby lowering all the available notes

Cup-shaped mouthpiece

REPTILE IMITATOR
It is obvious from its shape why this bizarre-looking instrument was called a serpent when it was invented in France in 1590. A cross between brass and woodwind, its snakelike tube had two sets of finger holes.

Left-hand finger holes

Placing one hand in the flared bell raises a note

Right-hand finger holes

EXTRA CURLS
During the 17th century, instrument makers gradually lengthened the horn and coiled it into a circle for ease of playing. But the range of notes the horn produced was still limited until a century later, when detachable sections of tubing were invented. Called crooks, these lengthened the tube and produced different sets of notes. This typical instrument has two crooks and dates from 1780.

Italian horn, c. 1720

Two ways of playing a serpent

Leather covering painted to resemble a serpent

Lizard-like creature carved into the wood.

Slender bell

RELIGIOUS MESSAGE
Fortunately for the player, this 5 ft (1.5 m) Moroccan trumpet is made in sections of brass that can be taken apart after use. It is called a *nfîr* and is used to signal the end of the Muslim fast of Ramadan with long blasts of sound. Trumpets like this date back to the Romans, who may have introduced them into North Africa.

MOUNTAIN MUSIC
The sound of the long, wooden alpenhorn has often echoed through the Alps of Switzerland. It was traditionally used by herders but today is played mainly for tourists.

Blazing brass

MODERN BRASS INSTRUMENTS IN FULL CRY, especially row after row of trumpets and trombones, can create a blaze of sound. This is not just because of the effort that goes into blowing them, although purple faces may well go along with a thrilling fanfare. The brilliant sound is due to the narrow metal tube, cylinder-shaped bore, and wide, flared bell. Brilliance of tone, however, is only half the story. Blowing softly produces a mellow sound; using a mute gives the music a hint of mystery or even menace. Jazz musicians make full use of the different moods that can be created by the trumpet and trombone, playing them with great individuality to create exciting solos.

HERALDIC FANFARE
The herald shown in this German print of c. 1600 is playing an early trumpet. The instrument had no valves at this time.

Piston valves

Cup-shaped mouthpiece

Bore widens after valves

LEADER OF THE BAND
The mellow tones of the brass band are topped by the cornet, which leads the band and plays solo passages. It was invented by adding valves to the coiled post horn (p. 20). The cornet produces the notes as the trumpet and is played in the same way. It makes a fatter, less piercing sound because the bore widens out more before the bell. But although the cornet may lack the trumpet's majesty, it is easier to play.

TRADITIONAL SETUP
Traditional jazz bands contain a trumpet and a trombone, as in Humphrey Lyttleton's band, shown here. Players aim to achieve a distinctively rough, growling sound.

SHOULDERING THE LOAD
The coils of this long and heavy 19th-century brass instrument enable the bandsman to carry it on his shoulder.

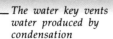

The water key vents water produced by condensation

Outer tube of slide

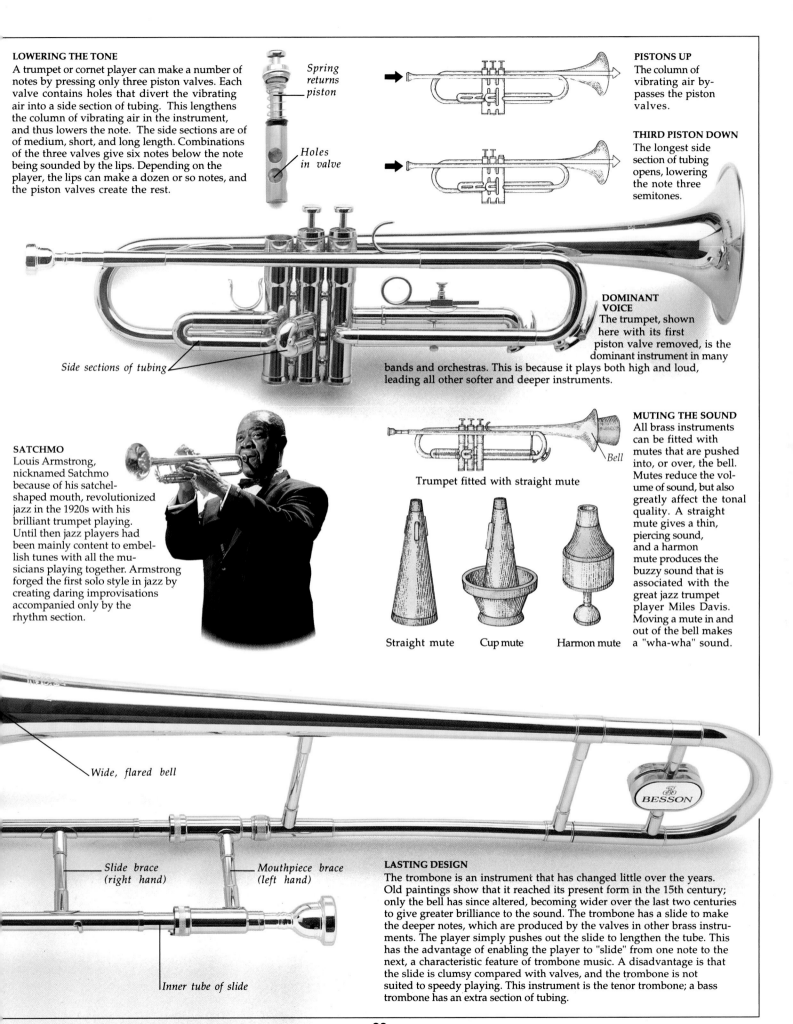

LOWERING THE TONE

A trumpet or cornet player can make a number of notes by pressing only three piston valves. Each valve contains holes that divert the vibrating air into a side section of tubing. This lengthens the column of vibrating air in the instrument, and thus lowers the note. The side sections are of medium, short, and long length. Combinations of the three valves give six notes below the note being sounded by the lips. Depending on the player, the lips can make a dozen or so notes, and the piston valves create the rest.

Spring returns piston

Holes in valve

PISTONS UP

The column of vibrating air by-passes the piston valves.

THIRD PISTON DOWN

The longest side section of tubing opens, lowering the note three semitones.

Side sections of tubing

DOMINANT VOICE

The trumpet, shown here with its first piston valve removed, is the dominant instrument in many bands and orchestras. This is because it plays both high and loud, leading all other softer and deeper instruments.

SATCHMO

Louis Armstrong, nicknamed Satchmo because of his satchel-shaped mouth, revolutionized jazz in the 1920s with his brilliant trumpet playing. Until then jazz players had been mainly content to embellish tunes with all the musicians playing together. Armstrong forged the first solo style in jazz by creating daring improvisations accompanied only by the rhythm section.

Bell

Trumpet fitted with straight mute

Straight mute   Cup mute   Harmon mute

MUTING THE SOUND

All brass instruments can be fitted with mutes that are pushed into, or over, the bell. Mutes reduce the volume of sound, but also greatly affect the tonal quality. A straight mute gives a thin, piercing sound, and a harmon mute produces the buzzy sound that is associated with the great jazz trumpet player Miles Davis. Moving a mute in and out of the bell makes a "wha-wha" sound.

Wide, flared bell

BESSON

Slide brace (right hand)

Mouthpiece brace (left hand)

Inner tube of slide

LASTING DESIGN

The trombone is an instrument that has changed little over the years. Old paintings show that it reached its present form in the 15th century; only the bell has since altered, becoming wider over the last two centuries to give greater brilliance to the sound. The trombone has a slide to make the deeper notes, which are produced by the valves in other brass instruments. The player simply pushes out the slide to lengthen the tube. This has the advantage of enabling the player to "slide" from one note to the next, a characteristic feature of trombone music. A disadvantage is that the slide is clumsy compared with valves, and the trombone is not suited to speedy playing. This instrument is the tenor trombone; a bass trombone has an extra section of tubing.

Curly horns and big tubas

A HOLLOW HORN was the ancestor of the horns that are now heard in orchestras and bands. The hollow sound of the horn - caused by the cone-shaped bore of the tube - means that it lacks the brilliance of the other principal brass instruments - the trumpet and trombone (pp. 22 - 23). Curly horns and a big tuba round out the sound of the brass section of a symphony orchestra, adding warmth and depth. The instruments require strong lips and lungs; the horn because it frequently has to produce high notes, the tuba because it is simply the most massive of all the wind instruments. In spite of the effort required to play these instruments, they can be played with great expression and sensitivity.

Rotary valves played by fingers of left hand

Wide, flared bell supported by right hand

Wide, cone-shaped bore gives mellow sound

Cup-shaped mouthpiece

DUAL NATIONALITY
The horn played in orchestras is often called the French horn, though in fact it developed mainly in Germany. This instrument is a double horn, and it is really two horns in one. The left thumb works a valve (p. 23) that switches between two sets of coiled tubing. One tube gives deep, warm notes, and the other gives high, bright notes. Straightened out, the double horn would be 30 ft (9 m) long!

The right hand fits inside the bell to adjust the notes

BRED FROM THE BUGLE
This tenor horn is a descendant of the bugle, on which soldiers sound calls to duty. Valves were added to the bugle in the 19th century, notably by the famous Adolphe Sax, better known for the saxophone (pp. 14 - 15). A whole family of horns, usually called saxhorns, resulted.

Piston valve

ON PARADE
Military bands make much use of brass instruments because they are easily carried on parade and make a loud, stirring sound. Here a line of cornets comes before a row of French horns. Military bands also contain woodwind instruments, such as clarinets and saxophones. Brass bands are normally limited to brass instruments, except for the bass drum which gives the beat.

HANDMADE HORNS
This 19th-century print of a horn factory in France shows the instruments being assembled. The horns were made in sections that were fitted together by hand.

24

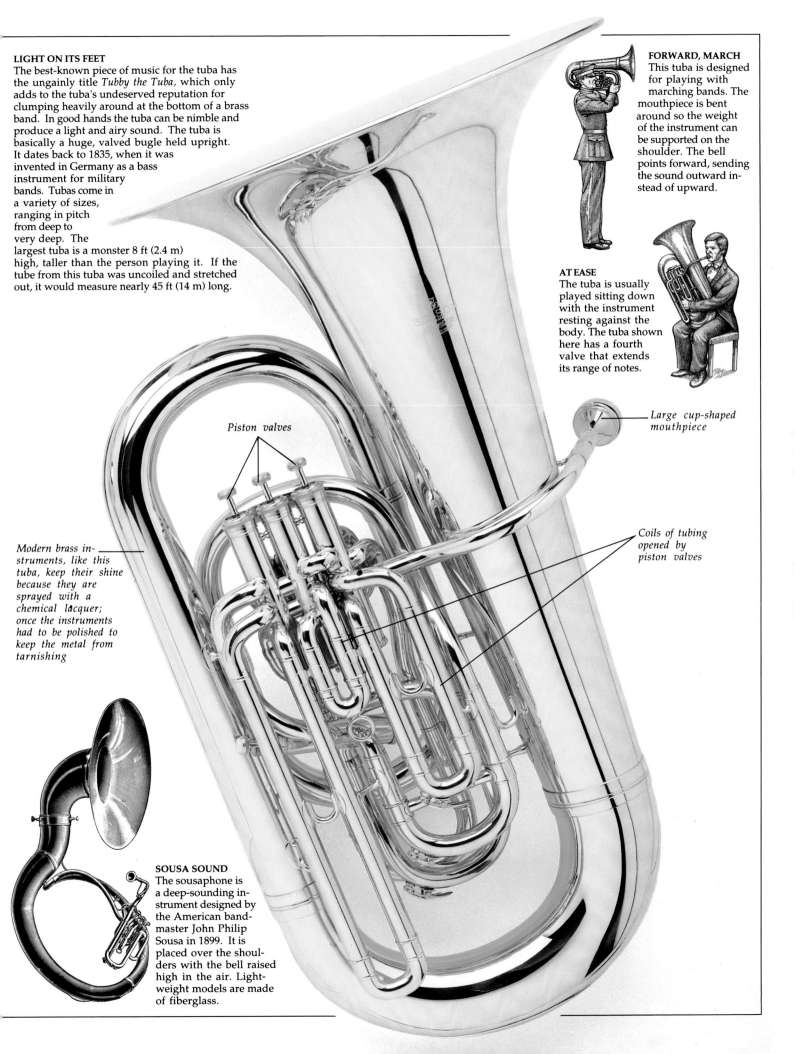

LIGHT ON ITS FEET
The best-known piece of music for the tuba has the ungainly title *Tubby the Tuba*, which only adds to the tuba's undeserved reputation for clumping heavily around at the bottom of a brass band. In good hands the tuba can be nimble and produce a light and airy sound. The tuba is basically a huge, valved bugle held upright. It dates back to 1835, when it was invented in Germany as a bass instrument for military bands. Tubas come in a variety of sizes, ranging in pitch from deep to very deep. The largest tuba is a monster 8 ft (2.4 m) high, taller than the person playing it. If the tube from this tuba was uncoiled and stretched out, it would measure nearly 45 ft (14 m) long.

FORWARD, MARCH
This tuba is designed for playing with marching bands. The mouthpiece is bent around so the weight of the instrument can be supported on the shoulder. The bell points forward, sending the sound outward instead of upward.

AT EASE
The tuba is usually played sitting down with the instrument resting against the body. The tuba shown here has a fourth valve that extends its range of notes.

Large cup-shaped mouthpiece

Piston valves

Coils of tubing opened by piston valves

Modern brass instruments, like this tuba, keep their shine because they are sprayed with a chemical lacquer; once the instruments had to be polished to keep the metal from tarnishing

SOUSA SOUND
The sousaphone is a deep-sounding instrument designed by the American bandmaster John Philip Sousa in 1899. It is placed over the shoulders with the bell raised high in the air. Lightweight models are made of fiberglass.

Breaking the silence

THE STUDY OF SOUND AND MUSIC began with notes plucked from a simple lyre in ancient Greece. Pythagoras (c. 582 - 507 B.C.), the famous scientist best known for squaring the hypotenuse, discovered that the pitch of a note created by a stretched string relates to the length of the string. If the lengths used are in simple proportions - such as 3 to 2, or 4 to 5 - then the notes which sound are in harmony. This principle lies behind all string instruments and, substituting air columns for strings, wind instruments (pp. 8- 9). Different notes can also be created by varying the tension and weight of the strings. The fingers of both hands make the sounds and create the notes in instruments like the violin, guitar, and sitar. Being able to influence both pitch and tone so directly gives the players great power of musical expression. This sensitivity partly explains why the violin family plays such an important part in classical music; their bowed strings produce a wonderful soaring sound when played in large groups. In the piano and harp, the fingers cannot affect the sound so much, but they make up for it because they have many more strings that can be played to sound chords and create cascades of notes.

MUSICAL WEIGHT
The strings on string instruments have to be strong to stand up to high tension and vibration when being played. They are most commonly made of nylon thread or steel wire.

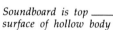

Soundboard is top surface of hollow body

F-shaped soundholes emit sound from inside the body

STRING SOUNDS

Stretched strings can be made to sound in three ways: by plucking them, as in the guitar; by bowing, as in the violin; and by hitting them, as in the piano. The whole string vibrates from one end to the other. Little sound comes from the vibrating strings, which cannot move much air to produce loud sound waves. The vibration spreads to a thin soundboard under, or at one end of, the strings. Made of springy, resilient wood, the soundboard vibrates strongly to make the sound of the instrument louder. The instrument, like this cello, may also have a hollow body that throbs as the air inside vibrates. Soundholes in the body allow this extra sound to escape. The simplest string instrument is no more than an archer's bow. To provide a resonating cavity, the musical bow may be held in the player's mouth.

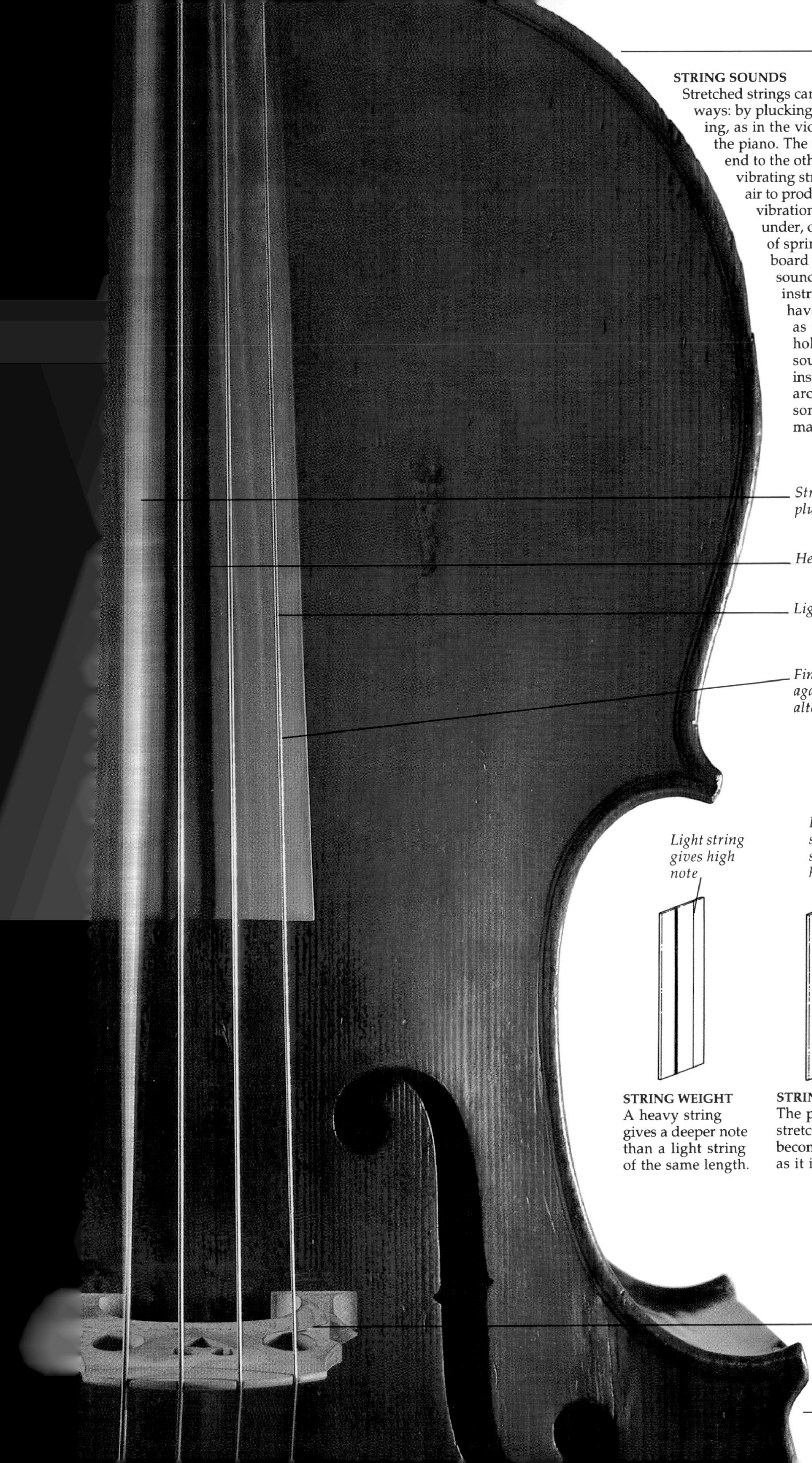

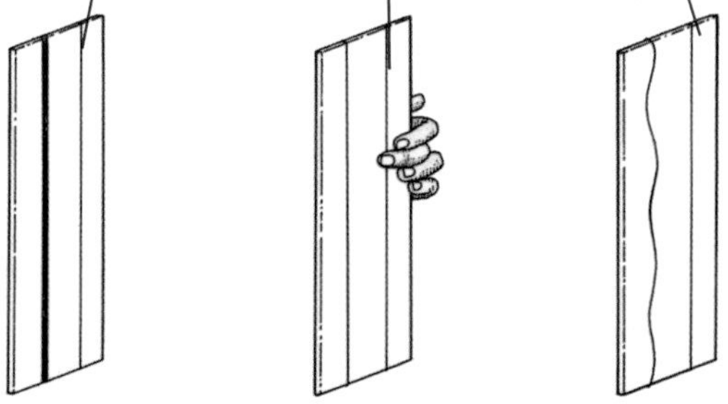

String vibrates when plucked or bowed

Heavy low string

Light high string

Fingers press strings against fingerboard to alter their length

Light string gives high note

Finger shortens string for high note

Increasing tension raises pitch

STRING WEIGHT
A heavy string gives a deeper note than a light string of the same length.

STRING LENGTH
The pitch of a stretched string becomes higher as it is shortened.

STRING TENSION
A tighter string gives a higher note than a looser string of the same length.

Bridge transmits vibration of strings to soundboard

Early and unusual strings

A cathedral wood carving of an angel with a "viol," c. 1390

MODERN BOWED STRING INSTRUMENTS are the result of many centuries of development. Their ancestors had a greater variety of features than modern standardized instruments, such as rounded or flat backs, fretted or fretless fingerboards, and varying numbers of strings including "sympathetic" strings. Playing techniques were different too; the smaller instruments were held vertically or against the chest instead of under the chin. Old features and techniques live on in folk instruments as well as revivals of ancient instruments.

The small, round-bodied rebec was an ancestor of the violin and was held horizontally and played with a bow.

Scroll with a carved lion's head

Ivory tuning peg

Plantlike patterns drawn in pen and ink

Carved head of a figure from mythology, possibly Ariadne; many instruments featured Cupid's head

MIDDLE-EASTERN SPLENDOR
The earliest bowed fiddles date back to the 10th century. This three-stringed spike fiddle was made in Iran in the 18th century. The spike extends from the ivory tuning pegs, passes through the neck, and then pierces the round body. The instrument is made of wood with a detailed inlay.

HORSE PLAY
The *morin-khuur*, a Mongolian fiddle, has a square body and an elegant, carved horse's head on the scroll.

Seven sympathetic strings lie beneath the seven melody strings

SCANDINAVIAN FOLK ART
This beautiful instrument is a folk fiddle of Norway. The decoration on the body is drawn in pen and ink, and the fingerboard is inlaid with bone and horn. Beneath the four strings that play melodies are four sympathetic strings. These are tuned to resonate (vibrate) as the melody strings sound. The fiddle became popular at Hardanger, Norway, in 1670 and this instrument dates from the mid-20th century.

Vellum (calfskin) head of soundbox

The spike passes right through the instrument

The spike is rested on the ground for playing

CUPID'S INFLUENCE
Viole d'amore ("love viol") seems a romantic name, but it refers to seven sympathetic strings that vibrate in sympathy with the seven melody strings. The strings and the shape of the body are similar to the viol but, like the viola (p. 30), it is held under the chin and has no frets. Vivaldi wrote for the viola d'amore, but its sound is too delicate for use in orchestras. This instrument was made in 1774.

*Neck and scroll
made of one piece
of wood*

*Miniature,
carved
head*

FAMILY TRAITS
Viols are a family of six-stringed instruments that have frets like the guitar (p. 42) but are played with a bow. This fine bass viol was made in Britain in 1713. It has frets made of gut that can be moved to adjust the tuning.

THE DANCING MASTER
The kit (right) was played by a dancing master as he demonstrated steps to his pupils. The fiddle was small enough to fit into the pocket, so in France the instrument was called a *pochette*, literally meaning "pocket." The bow could always be used, as shown in this late-18th-century engraving, to emphasize a point.

*Stroh violins
had only
one string*

*The amplifying horn
can be turned to project
the sound in the
required direction*

DANCING MINIATURE
The kit was a tiny fiddle that was popular during the 17th and 18th centuries. The round-bodied shape developed from the medieval rebec.

COUSIN OF
THE CELLO
This 16th-century Italian painting shows a bass viol with some of the features of the cello (p. 31), which developed at this time. It has f-shaped soundholes, for example.

PLAYING THE VIOL
Viols were played with the hand under the bow, which gave a very even sound that blended well. The three largest viols - the treble, tenor, and bass - were all played between the knees. They were popular until replaced by the violin family in the 18th century.

*Metal
amplifying
horn*

*C-shaped
soundhole
found on some
members of
the viol
family*

DESIGN CURIOSITY
The Stroh violin, or phonofiddle, was invented by the British musician Charles Stroh in 1901. Its single string caused a diaphragm at the side of the bridge to vibrate, and the horn enlarged the sound made by the diaphragm in the same way as an early phonograph. It was used in variety and music hall acts. Amplifying horns were also added to the side of some ordinary fiddles for use in early recording studios.

The violin family

THE VIOLIN achieved its present form in about 1550 and, together with the viola, cello, and double bass, developed to near perfection over the next two centuries. The rich and powerful sound, aided by playing techniques that gave greater expression, caused the violin family to replace the viols and other bowed strings. With the foundation of the symphony orchestra and string quartet in the 18th century, the violin family established a ruling position in Western classical music. The violin also invaded folk music; and the double bass, jazz.

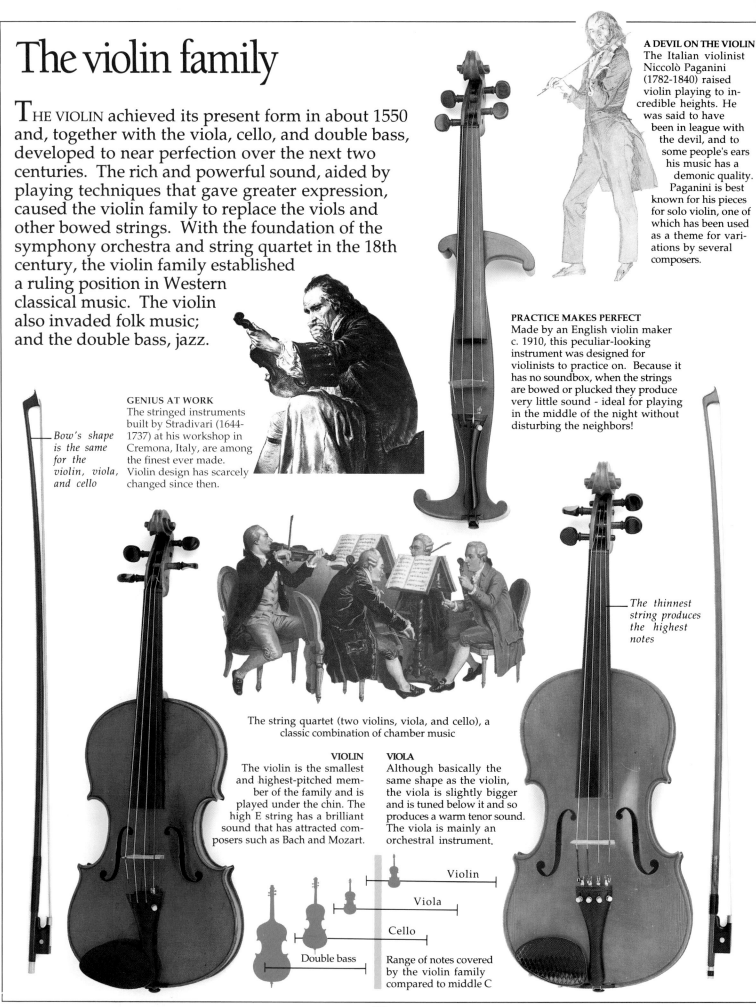

A DEVIL ON THE VIOLIN
The Italian violinist Niccolò Paganini (1782-1840) raised violin playing to incredible heights. He was said to have been in league with the devil, and to some people's ears his music has a demonic quality. Paganini is best known for his pieces for solo violin, one of which has been used as a theme for variations by several composers.

PRACTICE MAKES PERFECT
Made by an English violin maker c. 1910, this peculiar-looking instrument was designed for violinists to practice on. Because it has no soundbox, when the strings are bowed or plucked they produce very little sound - ideal for playing in the middle of the night without disturbing the neighbors!

Bow's shape is the same for the violin, viola, and cello

GENIUS AT WORK
The stringed instruments built by Stradivari (1644-1737) at his workshop in Cremona, Italy, are among the finest ever made. Violin design has scarcely changed since then.

The thinnest string produces the highest notes

The string quartet (two violins, viola, and cello), a classic combination of chamber music

VIOLIN
The violin is the smallest and highest-pitched member of the family and is played under the chin. The high E string has a brilliant sound that has attracted composers such as Bach and Mozart.

VIOLA
Although basically the same shape as the violin, the viola is slightly bigger and is tuned below it and so produces a warm tenor sound. The viola is mainly an orchestral instrument.

Violin

Viola

Cello

Double bass

Range of notes covered by the violin family compared to middle C

Each tuning
peg controls
one string

CELLO
The cello, or violon-
cello, is a low-pitched
instrument, its four
strings being tuned an
octave below the viola.
The cellist sits to play
it with the cello's body
resting on a metal
spike. It is an intensely
expressive instrument,
the high A string
having a wonderful
singing sound, and it is
often played solo.

The French bass
bow is held with
the fingers push-
ing down, as with a
violin or cello bow

The German bow has
a large frog (p. 33)
and is held with the
wrist upside down
and the thumb press-
ing down on the bow

DOUBLE BASS
The deepest member of the string family is the double
bass. Measuring about 6 ft (1.8 m) from scroll to spike,
this huge instrument rests on the floor with the
bass player standing behind. This double bass
has sloping shoulders (p. 29), unlike other
members of the violin family.
On some instruments a fifth
string may be added.
When the double
bass is plucked, it
produces a deep, res-
onant sound. It is
played rhythmi-
cally in this
way in jazz
and folk
music.

F-shaped sound-
hole typical of
violin family

Frog

Spike on which cello
rests on ground

Making a violin

THE CREATION OF A GOOD VIOLIN is a demanding art, for the instrument is virtually made by hand. Materials must be carefully chosen and months of toil go into the shaping, finishing, and assembly of the various parts. The end result is a beautiful instrument that is totally responsive to the player. The vibrations of the strings pass through the bridge into the hollow body. There they spread evenly and powerfully so that the body resonates to produce the rich, bright sound characteristic of the violin.

Violin-making methods have scarcely changed from the traditional skills used in this 18th-century workshop

Gouge

Thumb planes

Sections of maple for back

Belly ready for planing

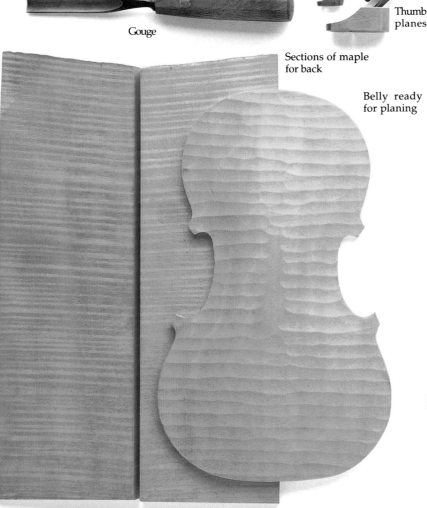

Purfling channel

Purfling made of mixed wood

CARVING THE BODY
A violin begins with sections of timber cut like slices of cake from a tree trunk. The wood must be both strong and springy to give the instrument a bright sound. A softwood such as pine or spruce is chosen for the front, or belly, of the body, and a hardwood, often maple, is used for the back. Each is usually formed of two sections glued together so that the grain runs evenly across it, although one-piece backs and, more rarely, fronts are sometimes seen. The outline of the belly or back is then marked on the glued sections using a template (pattern) and is carefully cut out with a fine saw. The wood is first carved into the approximate shape with a gouge. The violin maker then uses a series of small planes to smoothe away the gouge marks - the tiniest plane is about the size of a thumbnail. Delicate work is required, as even slight differences in the desired dimensions will change the violin's sound. The center of the plate is slightly rounded but the edges are flattened.

REFINING THE BODY
A special tool next cuts a narrow channel around the edge of the belly. A thin strip called the purfling is then inlaid into the channel. It is traditionally made of flexible layers of white maple and dyed pear wood. The purfling is decorative, but it also helps to keep the wood from splitting. The belly and back are then completed by carving the inside surface to shape. When finished, the belly has an even thickness of about .10 in (3 mm); the back is slightly thicker in the center.

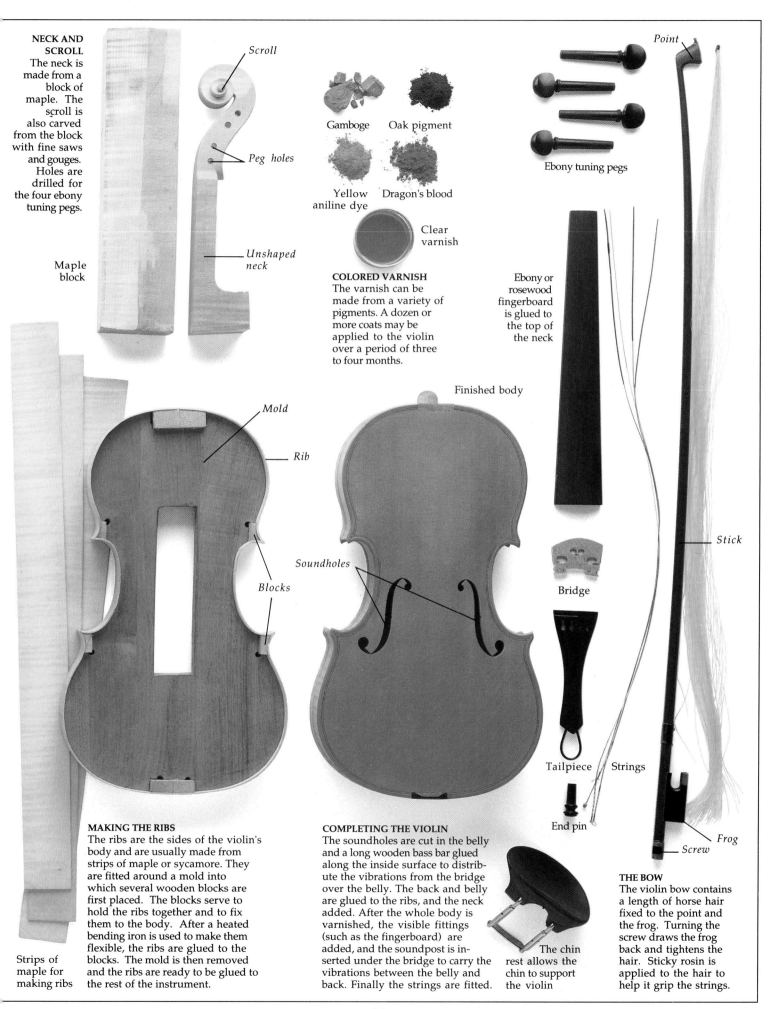

NECK AND SCROLL
The neck is made from a block of maple. The scroll is also carved from the block with fine saws and gouges. Holes are drilled for the four ebony tuning pegs.

Scroll

Peg holes

Unshaped neck

Maple block

Gamboge

Oak pigment

Yellow aniline dye

Dragon's blood

Clear varnish

COLORED VARNISH
The varnish can be made from a variety of pigments. A dozen or more coats may be applied to the violin over a period of three to four months.

Point

Ebony tuning pegs

Ebony or rosewood fingerboard is glued to the top of the neck

Finished body

Mold

Rib

Soundholes

Blocks

Bridge

Stick

Tailpiece

Strings

End pin

The chin rest allows the chin to support the violin

Frog

Screw

MAKING THE RIBS
The ribs are the sides of the violin's body and are usually made from strips of maple or sycamore. They are fitted around a mold into which several wooden blocks are first placed. The blocks serve to hold the ribs together and to fix them to the body. After a heated bending iron is used to make them flexible, the ribs are glued to the blocks. The mold is then removed and the ribs are ready to be glued to the rest of the instrument.

Strips of maple for making ribs

COMPLETING THE VIOLIN
The soundholes are cut in the belly and a long wooden bass bar glued along the inside surface to distribute the vibrations from the bridge over the belly. The back and belly are glued to the ribs, and the neck added. After the whole body is varnished, the visible fittings (such as the fingerboard) are added, and the soundpost is inserted under the bridge to carry the vibrations between the belly and back. Finally the strings are fitted.

THE BOW
The violin bow contains a length of horse hair fixed to the point and the frog. Turning the screw draws the frog back and tightens the hair. Sticky rosin is applied to the hair to help it grip the strings.

Harps and lyres

H<small>ARPS AND LYRES</small> are strongly associated with goodness: angels traditionally carry harps and the connection goes far back to the legend of Orpheus, who charmed all with his lyre. The instruments are in fact of ancient origin, and they appear all over the world. They consist basically of strings that stretch over a frame, and may have descended from the archer's bow. Most harps and lyres are plucked; some, like the Swedish *tallharper* still in use in Scandinavia, are played with a bow. The strings can each sound a different note and are often tuned to a scale of notes. The elegant concert harp makes a beautiful sound but is something of a beast to play - as well as having 47 strings to pluck, there are seven pedals that make different notes.

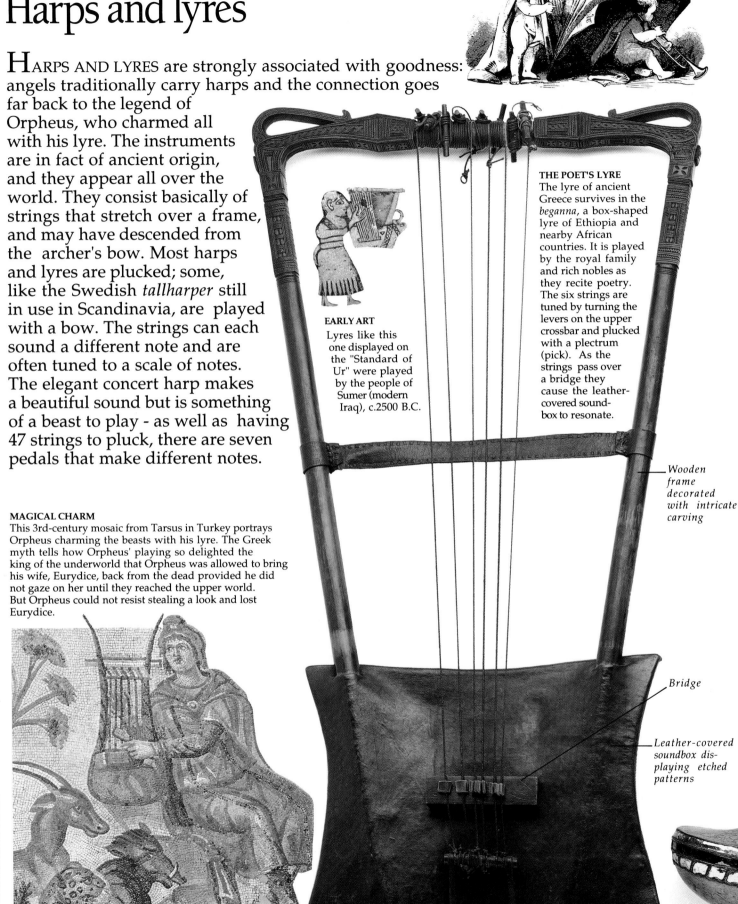

EARLY ART
Lyres like this one displayed on the "Standard of Ur" were played by the people of Sumer (modern Iraq), c.2500 B.C.

THE POET'S LYRE
The lyre of ancient Greece survives in the *beganna*, a box-shaped lyre of Ethiopia and nearby African countries. It is played by the royal family and rich nobles as they recite poetry. The six strings are tuned by turning the levers on the upper crossbar and plucked with a plectrum (pick). As the strings pass over a bridge they cause the leather-covered sound-box to resonate.

Wooden frame decorated with intricate carving

Bridge

Leather-covered soundbox displaying etched patterns

MAGICAL CHARM
This 3rd-century mosaic from Tarsus in Turkey portrays Orpheus charming the beasts with his lyre. The Greek myth tells how Orpheus' playing so delighted the king of the underworld that Orpheus was allowed to bring his wife, Eurydice, back from the dead provided he did not gaze on her until they reached the upper world. But Orpheus could not resist stealing a look and lost Eurydice.

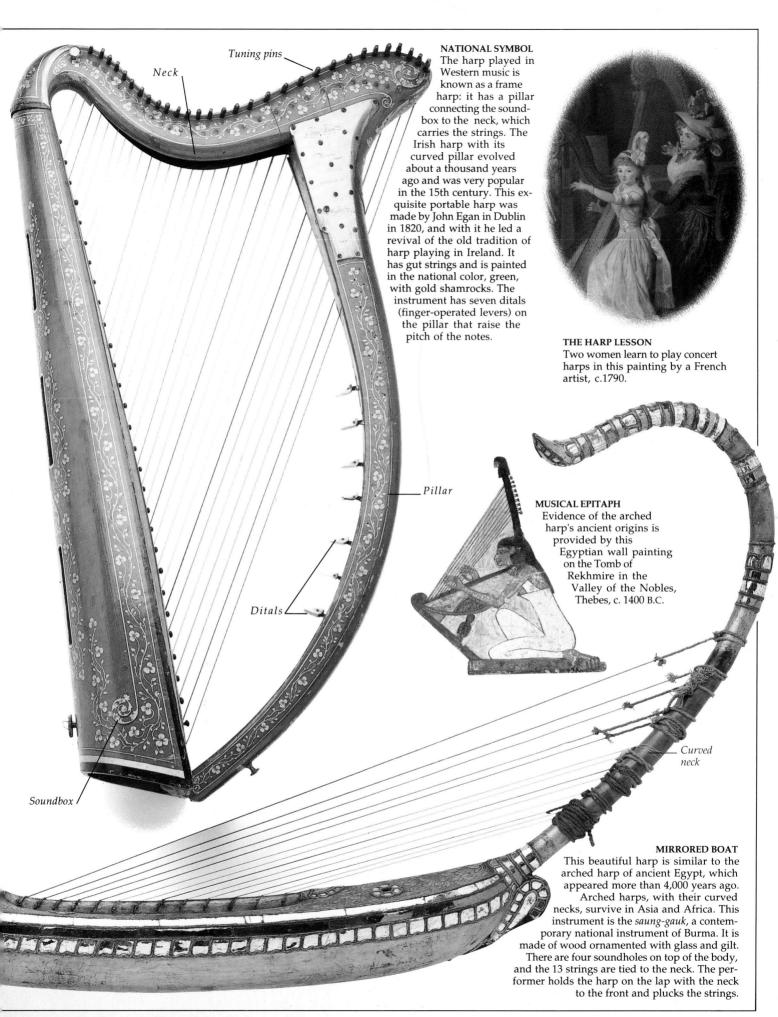

NATIONAL SYMBOL
The harp played in Western music is known as a frame harp: it has a pillar connecting the soundbox to the neck, which carries the strings. The Irish harp with its curved pillar evolved about a thousand years ago and was very popular in the 15th century. This exquisite portable harp was made by John Egan in Dublin in 1820, and with it he led a revival of the old tradition of harp playing in Ireland. It has gut strings and is painted in the national color, green, with gold shamrocks. The instrument has seven ditals (finger-operated levers) on the pillar that raise the pitch of the notes.

Neck

Tuning pins

Pillar

Ditals

Soundbox

THE HARP LESSON
Two women learn to play concert harps in this painting by a French artist, c.1790.

MUSICAL EPITAPH
Evidence of the arched harp's ancient origins is provided by this Egyptian wall painting on the Tomb of Rekhmire in the Valley of the Nobles, Thebes, c. 1400 B.C.

Curved neck

MIRRORED BOAT
This beautiful harp is similar to the arched harp of ancient Egypt, which appeared more than 4,000 years ago. Arched harps, with their curved necks, survive in Asia and Africa. This instrument is the *saung-gauk*, a contemporary national instrument of Burma. It is made of wood ornamented with glass and gilt. There are four soundholes on top of the body, and the 13 strings are tied to the neck. The performer holds the harp on the lap with the neck to the front and plucks the strings.

From pears to whole fishes

DATING BACK SOME 4,000 YEARS, the lute is the oldest ancestor of the violin and guitar. Like the guitar, the lute is plucked, and usually has frets. It can be distinguished from the guitar by its characteristic, half-pear-shaped body. Old lutes are recognizable because they often have a bewildering array of strings - some have as many as 13 pairs. Placing four fingers over them can be a struggle, and the lutenist probably spends more time tuning the instrument than playing it. This was one of the reasons why the lute fell from favor in Western music some two centuries ago.

17th-century musician with a *colascione*

SOLO ARMADILLO
The *charango* is a small South American lute, the back of which is made from the carapace (horny skin) of an armadillo. This instrument was made in Bolivia and has five pairs of strings. The armadillo is now protected, so most modern *charangos* have wooden backs.

Classic round-backed lute of the 15th century

ARAB ANCESTOR
The classical lute evolved from the *'ud*, an Arab lute that reached Europe in the 13th century. This Moroccan *'ud* is only about 40 years old. It has an S-shaped pegbox, and a deeper body and narrower neck than the classic lute, popular in Europe in the 15th and 16th centuries.

BENT OVER BACKWARD
Lute pegboxes bend back at a slight or steep angle. They may also have pairs of strings instead of single strings.

The armadillo carapace was dried in a mold to give it the right shape

Six-banded armadillo

Five pairs of open strings

Six pairs of strings and two single strings

HIGHLY STRUNG
This German baroque lute was made by Johann Christian Hoffmann, a friend of J.S. Bach, in the 18th century. It is a particular type of bass lute with two pegboxes. This one has 14 strings, stopped by the fingers on the unfretted fingerboard, and 10 open bass strings. It was used to play a continuo (bass line and chords) in the baroque music of the time.

Singing was often accompanied by a lute

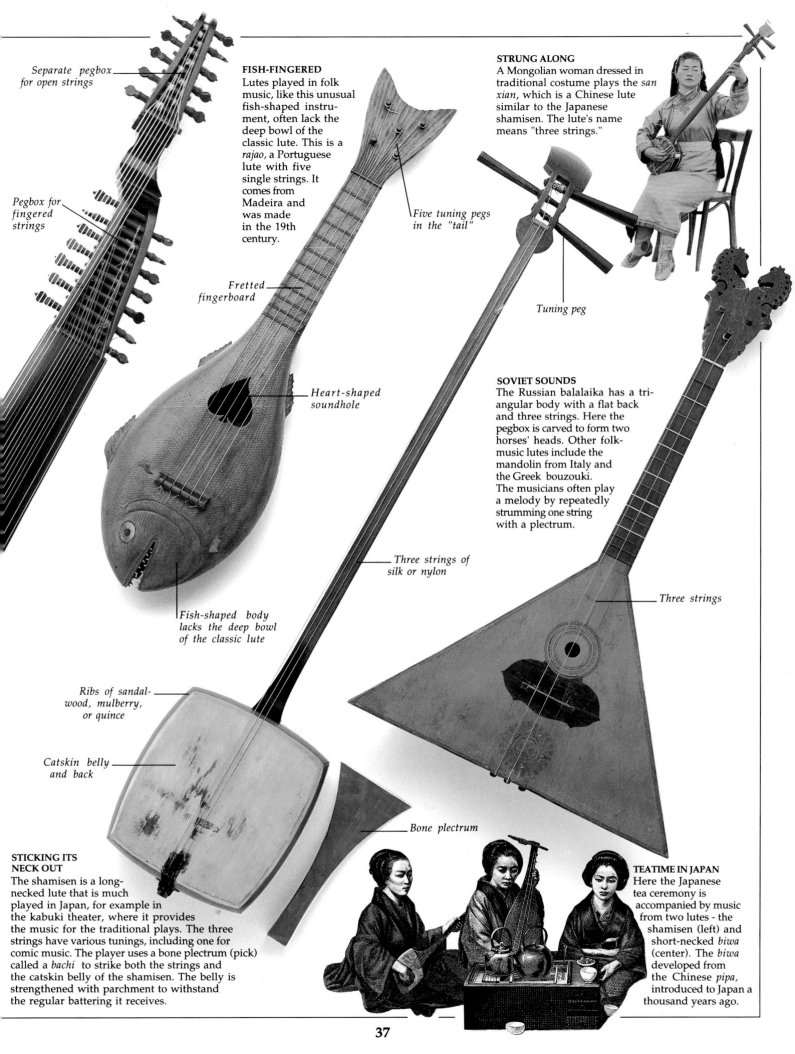

Separate pegbox
for open strings

Pegbox for
fingered
strings

FISH-FINGERED
Lutes played in folk
music, like this unusual
fish-shaped instru-
ment, often lack the
deep bowl of the
classic lute. This is a
rajao, a Portuguese
lute with five
single strings. It
comes from
Madeira and
was made
in the 19th
century.

Five tuning pegs
in the "tail"

Fretted
fingerboard

Heart-shaped
soundhole

STRUNG ALONG
A Mongolian woman dressed in
traditional costume plays the *san
xian*, which is a Chinese lute
similar to the Japanese
shamisen. The lute's name
means "three strings."

Tuning peg

SOVIET SOUNDS
The Russian balalaika has a tri-
angular body with a flat back
and three strings. Here the
pegbox is carved to form two
horses' heads. Other folk-
music lutes include the
mandolin from Italy and
the Greek bouzouki.
The musicians often play
a melody by repeatedly
strumming one string
with a plectrum.

Three strings of
silk or nylon

Fish-shaped body
lacks the deep bowl
of the classic lute

Three strings

Ribs of sandal-
wood, mulberry,
or quince

Catskin belly
and back

Bone plectrum

**STICKING ITS
NECK OUT**
The shamisen is a long-
necked lute that is much
played in Japan, for example in
the kabuki theater, where it provides
the music for the traditional plays. The three
strings have various tunings, including one for
comic music. The player uses a bone plectrum (pick)
called a *bachi* to strike both the strings and
the catskin belly of the shamisen. The belly is
strengthened with parchment to withstand
the regular battering it receives.

TEATIME IN JAPAN
Here the Japanese
tea ceremony is
accompanied by music
from two lutes - the
shamisen (left) and
short-necked *biwa*
(center). The *biwa*
developed from
the Chinese *pipa*,
introduced to Japan a
thousand years ago.

From gourd to board

LITTLE MATERIAL IS REQUIRED to make the ground zither of Africa and southeast Asia: dig a small pit in the ground and stretch a string across it; twang the string and the air in the pit vibrates with a note. This principle links all zithers that have strings stretched across a soundbox - plucking or beating the strings makes the soundbox resound with music. Zithers are popular in folk music, and in China the *qin* zither once held a privileged status and inspired philosophical theories. Zithers are quite easy to play, because you can make a tune simply by plucking the strings. Use two hands with a large set of strings, and a melody and accompaniment are possible. A fingerboard and frets enable a few melody strings to play a tune, while separate open strings provide the accompaniment.

Strips vibrate between bridges

Cane bridge

Hollow gourd resonates

STRIPS FOR STRINGS
In this raft zither from Nigeria (Africa), the strings are thin strips of cane cut from the body of the bamboo "raft."

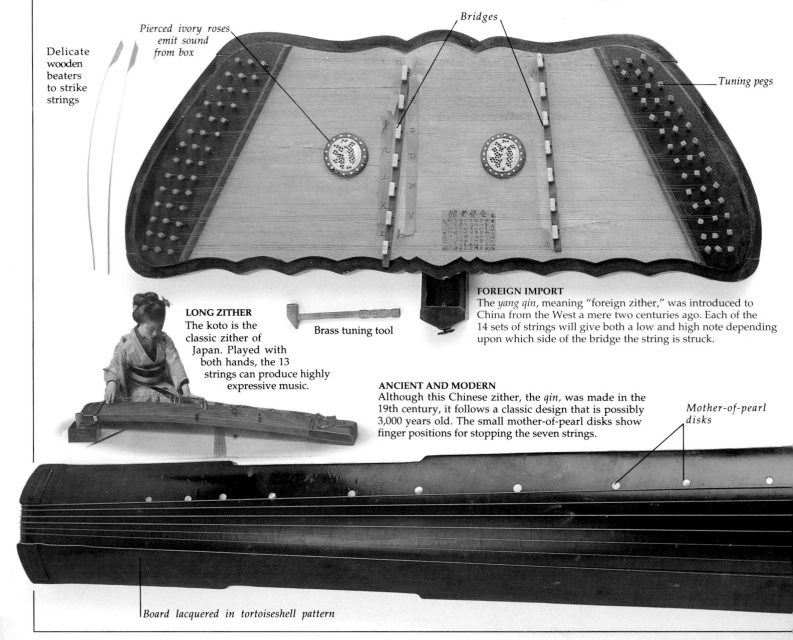

Delicate wooden beaters to strike strings

Pierced ivory roses emit sound from box

Bridges

Tuning pegs

LONG ZITHER
The koto is the classic zither of Japan. Played with both hands, the 13 strings can produce highly expressive music.

Brass tuning tool

FOREIGN IMPORT
The *yang qin*, meaning "foreign zither," was introduced to China from the West a mere two centuries ago. Each of the 14 sets of strings will give both a low and high note depending upon which side of the bridge the string is struck.

ANCIENT AND MODERN
Although this Chinese zither, the *qin*, was made in the 19th century, it follows a classic design that is possibly 3,000 years old. The small mother-of-pearl disks show finger positions for stopping the seven strings.

Mother-of-pearl disks

Board lacquered in tortoiseshell pattern

MUSICAL STICK
The principles that produce music from all hand-held string instruments can be seen in this *tzeze*, a simple stick zither from Uganda (Africa). A string is fixed to each end of the stick. Plucking with one hand sounds the string, which vibrates to make the gourd resonate. Pressing the fingers of the other hand against the frets shortens the string and varies the pitch of note being sounded.

SHAPELY PSALTERY
The psaltery was a 15th-century zither. It was sometimes made in unusual shapes - some were even shaped like a pig's head - with strings of different lengths. The psaltery developed from the *qanum*, a zither from the Middle East that reached Europe in the 11th century.

LUTELIKE ZITHER
The *bandura*, a traditional instrument of Ukraine, combines features of the zither and the lute (p. 36). It has melody strings stopped by the fingers on the double fingerboard, while the open strings are plucked to accompany the melody. This instrument, made in c. 1945, is intricately decorated with inlays and carved oak leaves.

TWANGING TUBE
The island of Madagascar, off the southeast coast of Africa, is the home of this simple tube zither, the *valiha*. The *valiha* is made from a piece of bamboo out of which strings have been cut and left attached at both ends. In order to allow the strings to vibrate, small pieces of wood have been inserted underneath. The player holds the tube upright, or under the arm, and plucks the taut strings with the fingers. Tube zithers can also be found in southeast Asia.

Inserted pieces of wood

Frets

Strings plucked by fingers

Hollow gourd

Stick

Double fingerboard

Inlay of zither player

Melody strings

Open strings

Mother-of-pearl inlay

Carved oak-leaf decoration

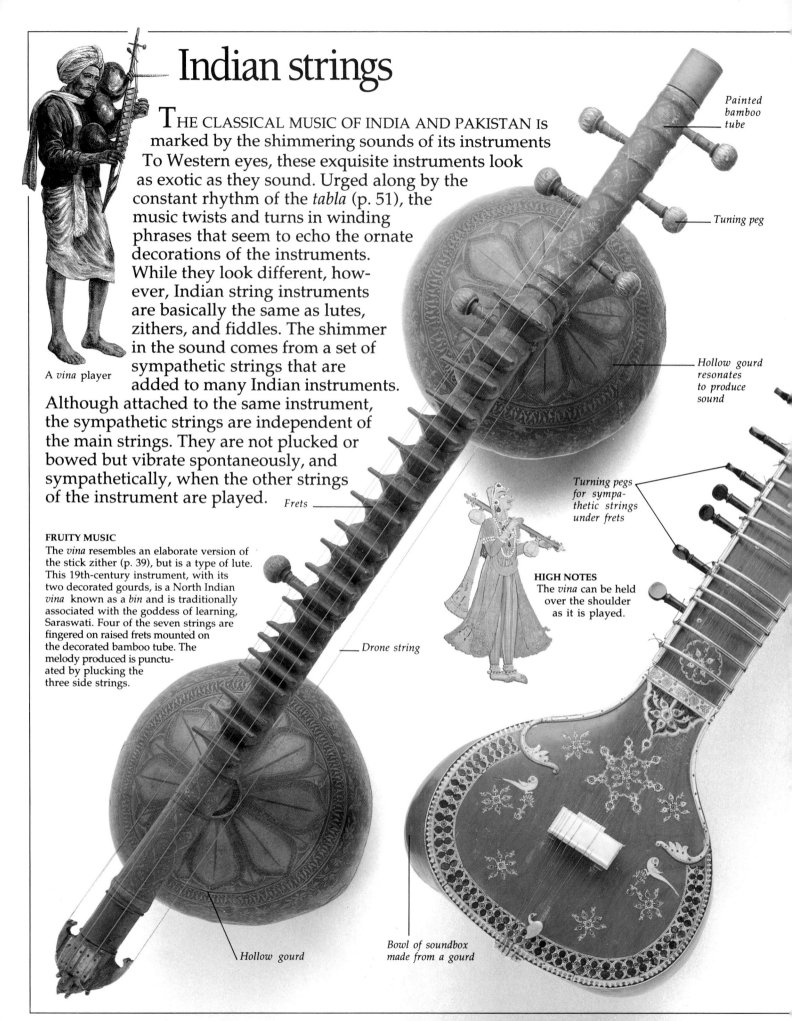

Indian strings

THE CLASSICAL MUSIC OF INDIA AND PAKISTAN is marked by the shimmering sounds of its instruments To Western eyes, these exquisite instruments look as exotic as they sound. Urged along by the constant rhythm of the *tabla* (p. 51), the music twists and turns in winding phrases that seem to echo the ornate decorations of the instruments. While they look different, however, Indian string instruments are basically the same as lutes, zithers, and fiddles. The shimmer in the sound comes from a set of sympathetic strings that are added to many Indian instruments. Although attached to the same instrument, the sympathetic strings are independent of the main strings. They are not plucked or bowed but vibrate spontaneously, and sympathetically, when the other strings of the instrument are played.

A *vina* player

Painted bamboo tube

Tuning peg

Hollow gourd resonates to produce sound

Frets

FRUITY MUSIC
The *vina* resembles an elaborate version of the stick zither (p. 39), but is a type of lute. This 19th-century instrument, with its two decorated gourds, is a North Indian *vina* known as a *bin* and is traditionally associated with the goddess of learning, Saraswati. Four of the seven strings are fingered on raised frets mounted on the decorated bamboo tube. The melody produced is punctuated by plucking the three side strings.

Turning pegs for sympathetic strings under frets

HIGH NOTES
The *vina* can be held over the shoulder as it is played.

Drone string

Hollow gourd

Bowl of soundbox made from a gourd

40

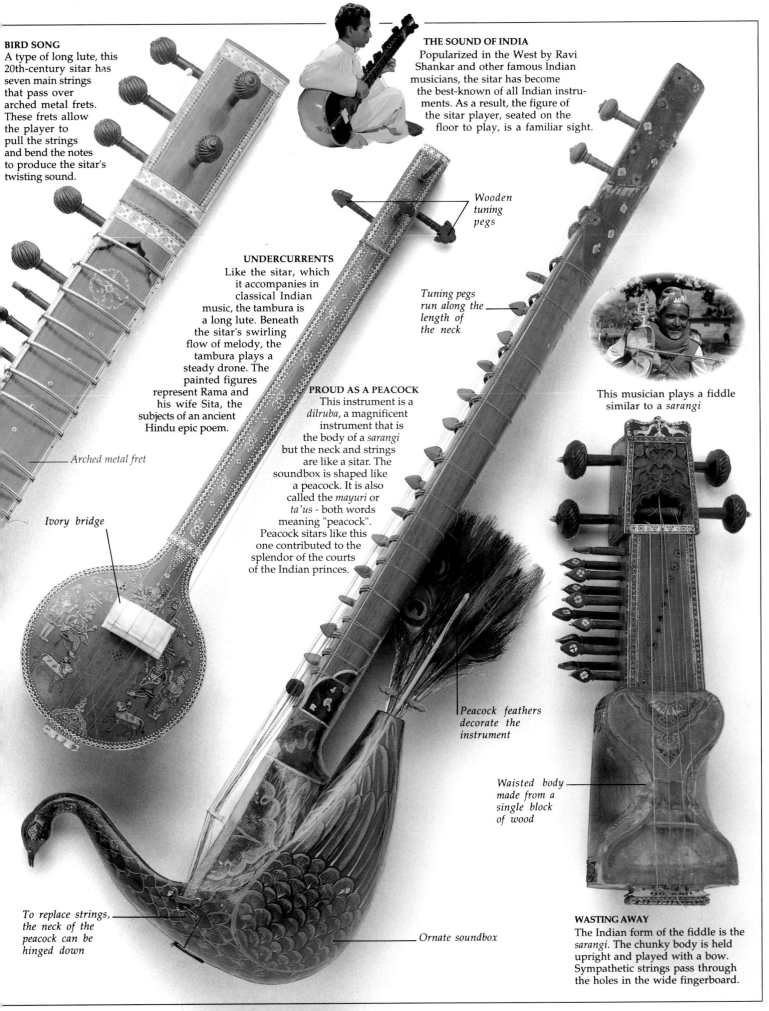

BIRD SONG
A type of long lute, this 20th-century sitar has seven main strings that pass over arched metal frets. These frets allow the player to pull the strings and bend the notes to produce the sitar's twisting sound.

THE SOUND OF INDIA
Popularized in the West by Ravi Shankar and other famous Indian musicians, the sitar has become the best-known of all Indian instruments. As a result, the figure of the sitar player, seated on the floor to play, is a familiar sight.

Wooden tuning pegs

UNDERCURRENTS
Like the sitar, which it accompanies in classical Indian music, the tambura is a long lute. Beneath the sitar's swirling flow of melody, the tambura plays a steady drone. The painted figures represent Rama and his wife Sita, the subjects of an ancient Hindu epic poem.

Tuning pegs run along the length of the neck

This musician plays a fiddle similar to a *sarangi*

Arched metal fret

PROUD AS A PEACOCK
This instrument is a *dilruba*, a magnificent instrument that is the body of a *sarangi* but the neck and strings are like a sitar. The soundbox is shaped like a peacock. It is also called the *mayuri* or *ta'us* - both words meaning "peacock". Peacock sitars like this one contributed to the splendor of the courts of the Indian princes.

Ivory bridge

Peacock feathers decorate the instrument

Waisted body made from a single block of wood

To replace strings, the neck of the peacock can be hinged down

Ornate soundbox

WASTING AWAY
The Indian form of the fiddle is the *sarangi*. The chunky body is held upright and played with a bow. Sympathetic strings pass through the holes in the wide fingerboard.

Creating a guitar

THE ACOUSTIC GUITAR IS FOREVER LINKED with Spain, so much so that it is often called the Spanish guitar. Flamenco, the folk music of Spain, is famous for its exciting guitar music as well as its energetic dancing. The instrument, with its body shaped like the figure 8, probably came to Spain from North Africa and may be descended from lutes like the 'ud (p. 36). By the 17th century, the guitar was being played all over Europe. Today acoustic and electric guitars (pp. 58-59) have spread throughout the world, and dominate popular music and much folk music in America and Europe.

This portrayal of a 19th-century Spanish guitar player shows the instrument in its present form

Top block joins the neck to the body

CLASSICAL GUITAR
This is the traditional form of the guitar, also known as the Spanish guitar. It has six strings, usually made of nylon, and a wide neck. The design dates back to the mid-19th century, when it was perfected by a Spanish carpenter named Antonio de Torres Jurado, often known simply as Torres. Guitars played in popular music usually have a finger plate fixed to the body to protect it.

Soundboard with struts for strength

Mold

Wooden linings are glued along top and bottom edges of ribs

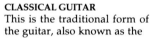

Flattop guitar with finger plate

Classical guitar

MAKING THE SOUNDBOARD
The most important part of the guitar is the soundboard – the front part of the body underneath the strings. It is made of two pieces of pine, spruce, cedar, or redwood that are glued together and then cut and shaped, or it may be made from layers of plywood. To strengthen the soundboard, struts are glued across the inside in a pattern that is crucial to the tone of the guitar. The sides, or ribs, of the guitar are made of two strips of rosewood, walnut, mahogany, maple, or sycamore. The strips are heated and shaped in a mold. Wooden blocks and linings are fixed to the inside of the ribs to make good joints for the soundboard and other parts.

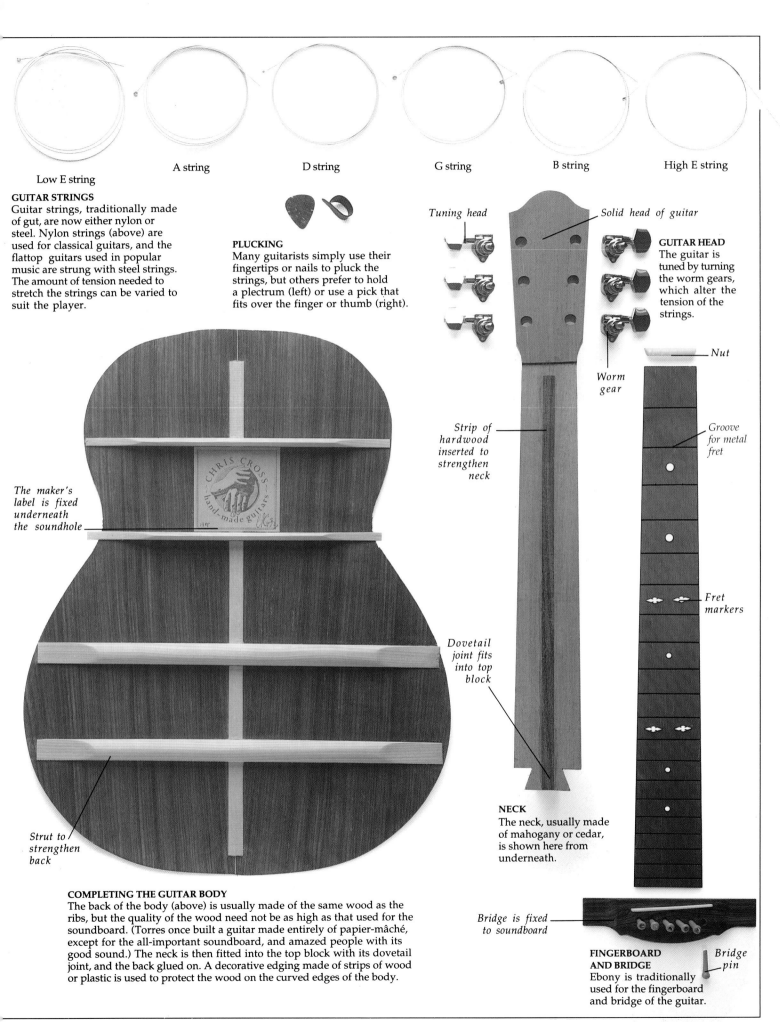

Low E string A string D string G string B string High E string

GUITAR STRINGS
Guitar strings, traditionally made of gut, are now either nylon or steel. Nylon strings (above) are used for classical guitars, and the flattop guitars used in popular music are strung with steel strings. The amount of tension needed to stretch the strings can be varied to suit the player.

PLUCKING
Many guitarists simply use their fingertips or nails to pluck the strings, but others prefer to hold a plectrum (left) or use a pick that fits over the finger or thumb (right).

Tuning head

Solid head of guitar

GUITAR HEAD
The guitar is tuned by turning the worm gears, which alter the tension of the strings.

Worm gear

Nut

The maker's label is fixed underneath the soundhole

CHRIS CROSS
hand-made guitars

Strip of hardwood inserted to strengthen neck

Groove for metal fret

Fret markers

Dovetail joint fits into top block

NECK
The neck, usually made of mahogany or cedar, is shown here from underneath.

Strut to strengthen back

COMPLETING THE GUITAR BODY
The back of the body (above) is usually made of the same wood as the ribs, but the quality of the wood need not be as high as that used for the soundboard. (Torres once built a guitar made entirely of papier-mâché, except for the all-important soundboard, and amazed people with its good sound.) The neck is then fitted into the top block with its dovetail joint, and the back glued on. A decorative edging made of strips of wood or plastic is used to protect the wood on the curved edges of the body.

Bridge is fixed to soundboard

FINGERBOARD AND BRIDGE
Ebony is traditionally used for the fingerboard and bridge of the guitar.

Bridge pin

Keynotes

 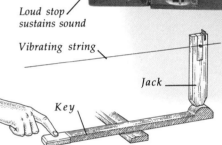

Mastering numerous strings, like those of the zither (p.38), can be a problem. The solution to tattered and tangled fingers came with the addition of a keyboard in the 15th century. Keyboards had been used to sound sets of pipes in organs (p.18) for centuries. But using them to sound strings led to the development of domestic instruments with greater powers of expression. In the spinet, virginal, and the larger harpsichord, the keys worked a mechanism to pluck the strings. Their limited range of volume, however, led to the invention of the piano, a keyboard instrument that hammered the strings to play both soft and loud, or, in Italian *piano* and *forte*.

PAINTED VIRGINAL
This 17th-century painting by the Dutch artist Vermeer shows a young girl seated at the keyboard of a virginal. The lid of her beautifully decorated instrument is lifted to reveal a painted landscape. The shape of the case means that the strings of this virginal run almost parallel to the keyboard.

Loud stop sustains sound

Vibrating string

Jack

Key

KEY PRESSED
Pressing the key of a spinet, virginal, or harpsichord raises a wooden jack with a quill or plectrum that plucks the string.

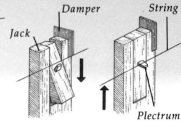

Damper

String

Jack

Plectrum

KEY RETURNS
The plectrum pivots away from the string as the damper falls.

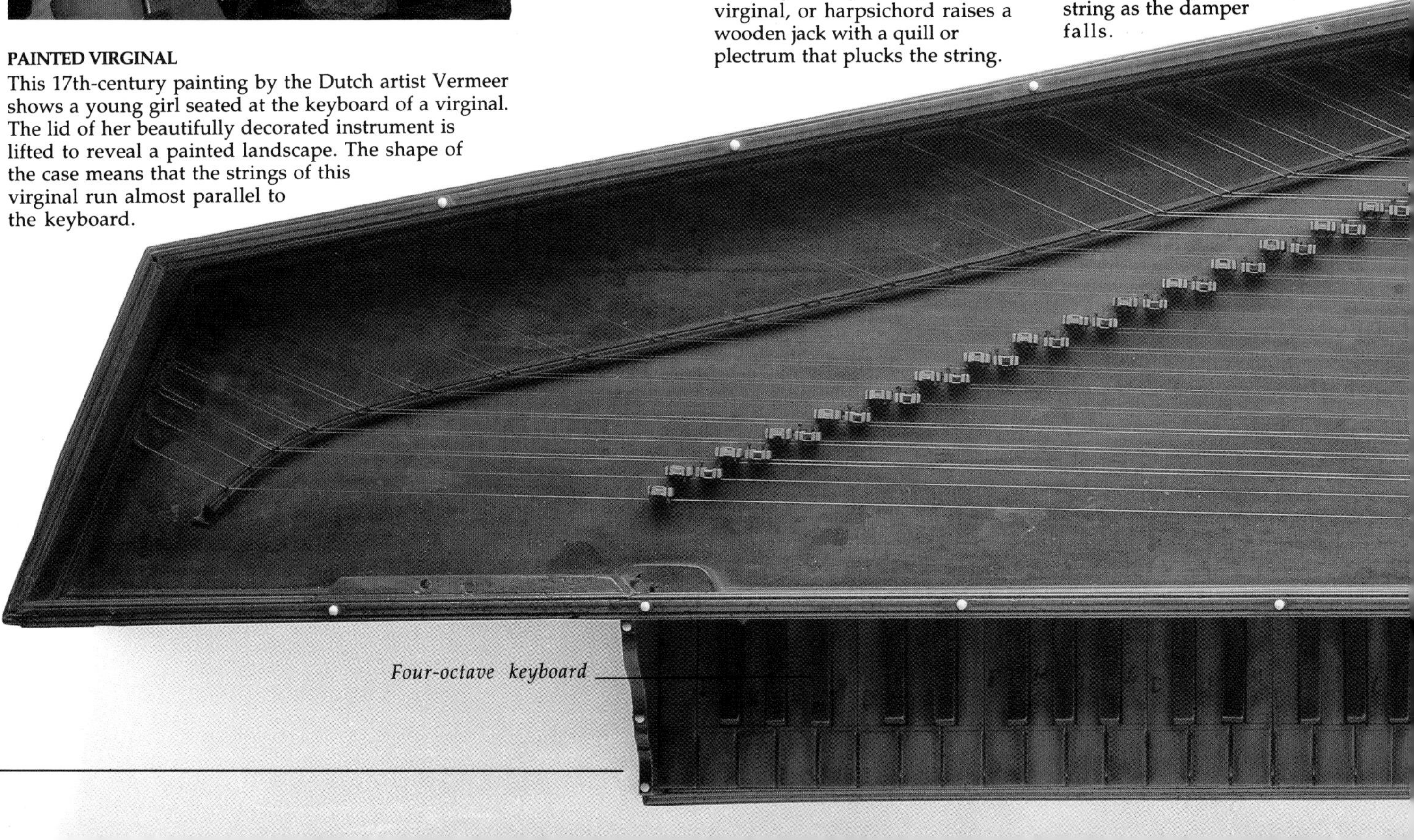

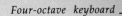

Four-octave keyboard

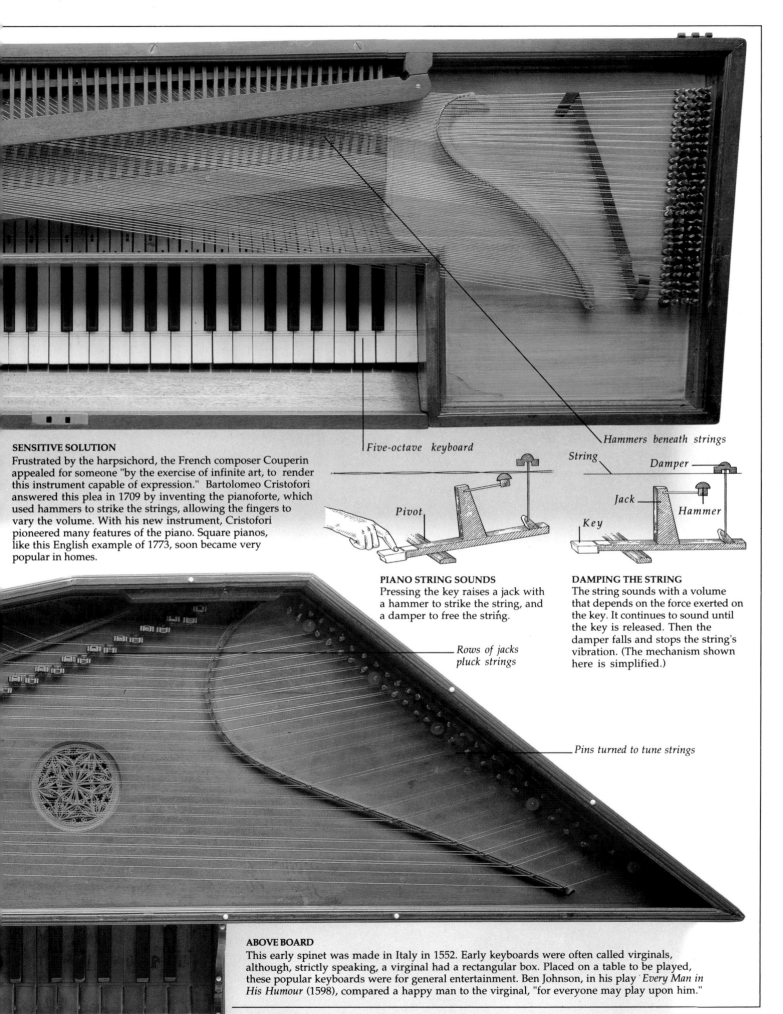

SENSITIVE SOLUTION

Frustrated by the harpsichord, the French composer Couperin appealed for someone "by the exercise of infinite art, to render this instrument capable of expression." Bartolomeo Cristofori answered this plea in 1709 by inventing the pianoforte, which used hammers to strike the strings, allowing the fingers to vary the volume. With his new instrument, Cristofori pioneered many features of the piano. Square pianos, like this English example of 1773, soon became very popular in homes.

Five-octave keyboard

Pivot

Hammers beneath strings

String

Damper

Jack

Hammer

Key

PIANO STRING SOUNDS
Pressing the key raises a jack with a hammer to strike the string, and a damper to free the string.

Rows of jacks pluck strings

DAMPING THE STRING
The string sounds with a volume that depends on the force exerted on the key. It continues to sound until the key is released. Then the damper falls and stops the string's vibration. (The mechanism shown here is simplified.)

Pins turned to tune strings

ABOVE BOARD

This early spinet was made in Italy in 1552. Early keyboards were often called virginals, although, strictly speaking, a virginal had a rectangular box. Placed on a table to be played, these popular keyboards were for general entertainment. Ben Johnson, in his play *Every Man in His Humour* (1598), compared a happy man to the virginal, "for everyone may play upon him."

Grand and upright

Bass notes have thick single strings about the same length as the medium strings

NO OTHER SOLO INSTRUMENT has the power of the piano, which can respond so readily to the touch of the fingers. The ability to play a different note with each finger, and to make each note soft or loud, gives the piano a tremendous range of expression. A pianist can produce magnificent music either alone or with the accompaniment of an orchestra. The piano is also important in popular music and jazz, where it can dominate or support other instruments. The best pianos are grand pianos, and they are "grand" in both size and sound. Upright pianos are more common because they take up less floor space and are less expensive. A good upright piano should maintain the full and bright sound of the grand piano, despite its size and shape.

The composer and virtuoso pianist Franz Liszt in 1824

PIANO IN THE PARLOR
The piano was more popular a century ago, before the gramophone and radio brought music into the home. People would gather around the piano for a sing-along and guest houses advertised the presence of a piano as motels now advertise cable television.

Wooden case

Soundboard of pine, spruce, or similar wood

Treble notes each have three strings to make them sound louder

CASE HISTORY
This grand piano of 1878 is typically ornate, but its overall shape has not changed since the piano was invented in 1709. The case is shaped to contain the long brass strings, and curves in for the shorter treble strings.

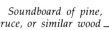

HIGH TENSION
All pianos contain an iron frame on which the metal strings are stretched with great force. Pressing the keys makes felt-tipped hammers strike the strings, which vibrate. This causes the soundboard underneath the strings to resonate, making the piano's distinctive sound.

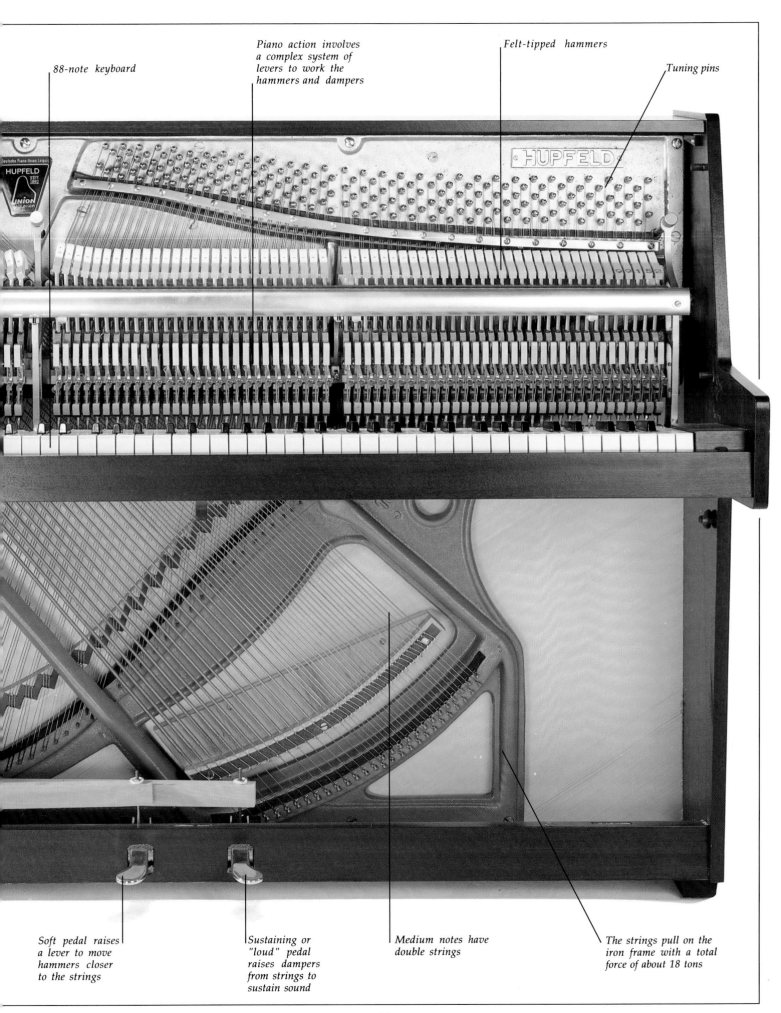

88-note keyboard

Piano action involves a complex system of levers to work the hammers and dampers

Felt-tipped hammers

Tuning pins

Soft pedal raises a lever to move hammers closer to the strings

Sustaining or "loud" pedal raises dampers from strings to sustain sound

Medium notes have double strings

The strings pull on the iron frame with a total force of about 18 tons

47

Musical impact

MUSIC HAS TO BE COAXED from many instruments: a violin must be fingered with skill, a flute blown with sensitivity. Few such requirements apparently apply to percussion instruments. Just hit them, shake them, scrape them, and out come the sounds. But playing percussion is not quite so simple. Exactly the right amount of force must be used to set the instrument vibrating in the right way. The stretched skin in the head of a drum has to vibrate to set the air inside ringing with sound. A smaller or tighter head makes a higher note, following the same principle as a stretched string (pp. 26-27). Orchestral timpani, or kettle-drums, are tuned to certain notes in this way. In other percussion instruments, such as cymbals and rattles, the whole body of the instrument may vibrate to give out sound. Tuned percussion instruments like the xylophone make definite notes; bars or bells of different sizes are struck to ring out the notes.

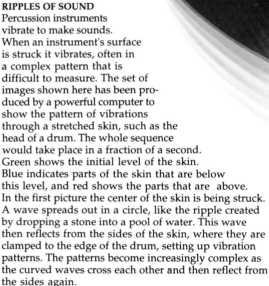

The edges of the cymbal vibrate so fast that they make a blur

1

2

RIPPLES OF SOUND
Percussion instruments vibrate to make sounds. When an instrument's surface is struck it vibrates, often in a complex pattern that is difficult to measure. The set of images shown here has been produced by a powerful computer to show the pattern of vibrations through a stretched skin, such as the head of a drum. The whole sequence would take place in a fraction of a second. Green shows the initial level of the skin. Blue indicates parts of the skin that are below this level, and red shows the parts that are above. In the first picture the center of the skin is being struck. A wave spreads out in a circle, like the ripple created by dropping a stone into a pool of water. This wave then reflects from the sides of the skin, where they are clamped to the edge of the drum, setting up vibration patterns. The patterns become increasingly complex as the curved waves cross each other and then reflect from the sides again.

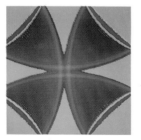

3

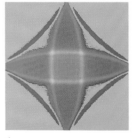

4

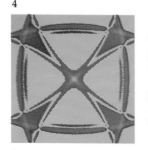

5

6

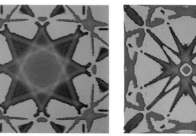

7

8

GOOD VIBRATIONS
A cymbal is a thin disk of
bronze held at the center so that the
edges are free to vibrate. Striking the cymbal
with a stick makes it sound with a loud crash.
The impact causes the metal disk to distort slightly, but because it is flexible, it immediately snaps back and sets the whole disk flexing back and forth
in a similar way to a drum skin (left). It takes some time for these
vibrations to die out. Striking the cymbal in different places varies the
sound, because different kinds of vibration patterns are set up.

*Thin bronze disk
clamped at the center*

Rhythm and ritual

African drum suspended from neck

APART FROM the physical effort that goes into beating a drum, the music often gathers its own energy as strong rhythms seem to drive it forward. A vitality is created that sets bodies swaying, hands clapping, and feet tapping. Shaking rattles and scraping instruments often help to whip up the energy of the music. Music, however, is not the sole purpose of these instruments. Drums and rattles have always played an important part in rituals, and "talking" drums can even send messages far afield.

Young boy playing a pair of African conical drums

SHAKE, RATTLE, AND ROLL
These small drums are half drum and half rattle. Twirling the handle vigorously causes the beads on the cords to fly back and forth and strike the drum-heads with a rattling sound. Glass beads, pellets of wax, or just knots in the cords may be used. The Chinese *t'ao-ku* with its five drums dates back around 3,000 years. The other instrument is from India. Rattle drums, also called clapper drums or pellet drums, are common in Asia. They are used as toys or by street vendors to attract attention.

Indian rattle drum

Chinese rattle drum

Wooden body inlaid with tortoiseshell and mother-of-pearl

The skin is struck with the fingers or a curved stick

Pressing the cords increases the tension of the skins in the two heads and raises the notes

DANCE RHYTHM
The tabor was the most common drum in 15th-century Europe and was often used to lead the dancing. The musician would beat on the drum with a stick held in one hand while playing a pipe held in the other hand.

MARCHING DRUM
Military bands contain many drums that play a constant rhythm to which the soldiers can march in step. The drums are carried on a sling around the body so that the drummer can walk.

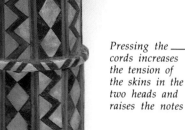

DRINKING DRUM
Goblet drums - single-headed drums in the shape of a goblet - are popular in Arab countries. This example is an Egyptian *darabuka*. The "goblet" is made of pottery or wood. The drum is struck at the center and edges of the skin with two hands.

BEATING WORDS
This *kalengo* from Nigeria is famous for its ability to "talk." By pressing the cords on this waisted drum, the drummer can raise and lower each note. The drum makes the sound of a tonal African language.

CLASPING AT CORDS
The *tsuzumi* is a small, waisted drum played in Japan. The cords that join the wide heads are gripped with one hand, which squeezes or releases the cords to vary the note.

Rattles

A rattle is simply shaken to make a sound. Many cultures used the rattle as part of traditional rituals, often to emphasize dance movements. Some rattles are simply strings of small, hard objects such as shells; others are made from pebbles, beads, and seeds inside a container.

ON THE OUTSIDE
This Nigerian rattle has strings of pellets fixed to the outside of a gourd.

HEAD SHAKER
Carved in the form of a human skull, this gruesome wooden rattle comes from North America.

DRIVING FORCE
The *tabla* is one of a pair of drums that drive along the sitar and tambura (pp. 40-41) in Indian music. The *tabla* player hits the center of the skin with the fingers while pressing down with the palm of the hand to vary the note.

RATTLE ON A STICK
Fruit shells filled with stones and mounted on a long stick make up this South African rattle.

MUSICAL OIL DRUM
Traditionally, the West Indian steel drum is made from an oil drum. Instead of a taut skin, it has a curved metal pan containing several panels that sound a different note when struck. A band contains a set of pans.

Metal jingle

Kapchen (skin-covered stick) used to beat *nungu*

MAGIC JINGLES
This unusual drum, seen from below, is the *nungu* from Siberia. The curious bits and pieces that hang from the bar are called *kungru*, and they jingle when the drum is beaten, like a tambourine. The *nungu* was played by a shaman, a priest whose magical powers depended on the number of *kungru*. The skin of the drum is decorated with red patterns that represent the upper and lower worlds. A drum in which a skin is stretched over a simple open frame like this is called a frame drum.

Nungu

On the beat

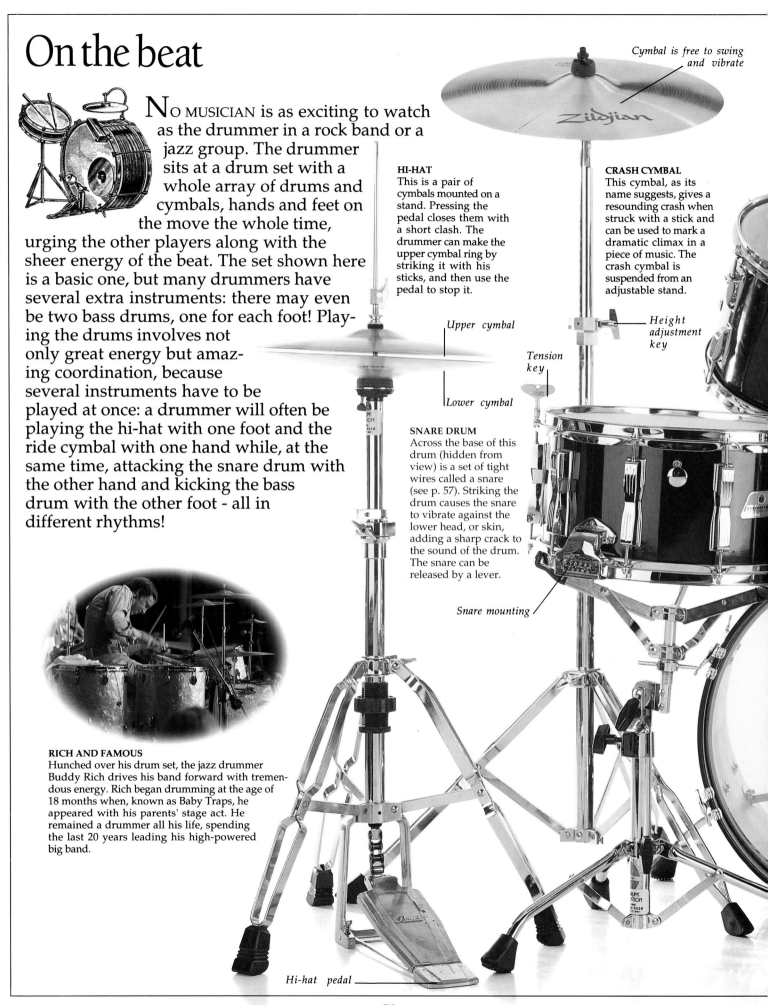

No MUSICIAN is as exciting to watch as the drummer in a rock band or a jazz group. The drummer sits at a drum set with a whole array of drums and cymbals, hands and feet on the move the whole time, urging the other players along with the sheer energy of the beat. The set shown here is a basic one, but many drummers have several extra instruments: there may even be two bass drums, one for each foot! Playing the drums involves not only great energy but amazing coordination, because several instruments have to be played at once: a drummer will often be playing the hi-hat with one foot and the ride cymbal with one hand while, at the same time, attacking the snare drum with the other hand and kicking the bass drum with the other foot - all in different rhythms!

RICH AND FAMOUS
Hunched over his drum set, the jazz drummer Buddy Rich drives his band forward with tremendous energy. Rich began drumming at the age of 18 months when, known as Baby Traps, he appeared with his parents' stage act. He remained a drummer all his life, spending the last 20 years leading his high-powered big band.

HI-HAT
This is a pair of cymbals mounted on a stand. Pressing the pedal closes them with a short clash. The drummer can make the upper cymbal ring by striking it with his sticks, and then use the pedal to stop it.

Upper cymbal

Lower cymbal

SNARE DRUM
Across the base of this drum (hidden from view) is a set of tight wires called a snare (see p. 57). Striking the drum causes the snare to vibrate against the lower head, or skin, adding a sharp crack to the sound of the drum. The snare can be released by a lever.

Snare mounting

Cymbal is free to swing and vibrate

CRASH CYMBAL
This cymbal, as its name suggests, gives a resounding crash when struck with a stick and can be used to mark a dramatic climax in a piece of music. The crash cymbal is suspended from an adjustable stand.

Height adjustment key

Tension key

Hi-hat pedal

CAUGHT IN THE ACT
As this picture was taken, the drummer played a fast roll along four tom-toms mounted on a pair of bass drums. A rapidly repeating camera flash shows the sticks in action, revealing how evenly the drummer played.

Adjustable damper varies length of sound

TWO TOM-TOMS
Two tom-toms, or "toms," are mounted on the top of the bass drum. These small drums give high-pitched, mellow notes. They have a single head, which may be damped.

FLOOR TOM
This large tom-tom gives a deep, resonant note. The drummer may use mallets to play the tom-toms or strike them with the palms of the hands.

RIDE CYMBAL
This cymbal is often played with a stick to produce a "riding" rhythm.

Stick

Mallet

Brush (wire or plastic bristles)

BEATERS AND BRUSHES
Drummers mainly use sticks, brushes, or mallets to play the drums and cymbals. Sticks and mallets give the loudest sound, and brushes are quiet.

BASS DRUM
The bass drum lies on its side and is played with a pedal connected to a felt-covered beater. It gives a short, deep thud.

Bass drum pedal

Rubber feet grip floor firmly

Appeal of percussion

NOTES as well as noises can ring out from percussion instruments. Striking bells of various sizes, or bars of wood or metal, gives a whole set of notes. Belltowers and carillons, which are the biggest instruments of all, send peals of notes and tunes pouring down to the streets below. At the other end of the scale, a few bars laid on a frame, or even across the player's legs, produce lovely chiming sounds, resounding with music that is both tuneful and rhythmic at the same time.

Wooden beater

TWO-TONE
This double bell comes from West Africa. It is made of metal covered with fabric. The bells give two different notes when struck by the wooden beater.

CHINESE CHIMES
Chimes go back to the Stone Age, when they were made from stone slabs. Shown here is a *po-chung*, from China. The bell is part of a chime - a group of bells suspended from a frame and struck with a stick. Seen as symbols of fertility, the bells were once used in temple ceremonies. Different notes were sounded to mark the seasons of the year.

Suspending chain

Raised studs represent nipples

Chime of gongs from Burma

BEATING THE BOSS
Unlike a bell, which produces the greatest vibrations when struck around the rim, the gong is suspended from its rim and struck at the center. The swoosh of sound then vibrates from the central "boss" to the edges of the gong. While it may provide a signal - if only to dine - in orchestral music a gong is an omen of doom. Gongs are popular in southeast Asia, and this elaborate example, decorated with fantastic beasts, comes from Borneo. They are often played in sets like the circular chimes of Thailand and Burma.

Suspending cord

Beater with cork head

Central boss struck by beater

Leather strap is gripped in one hand

Clapper

HANDY CLANGERS
Handbells have been popular since the 12th century. These two come from a set of bells, each tuned to a different note of the scale. The bells contain a clapper that strikes the rim, making it vibrate with a clang. Groups of bell ringers play the bells by ringing in order.

High temple block

Medium temple block

Low temple block

Beaters

Carved wooden fishes

CEASELESS PRAYERS
Originating in China, these instruments are called *mu-yus*, which means "wooden fish." Carved to resemble fishes, the *mu-yu* is symbolic of ceaseless prayer, because fish never seem to sleep. They are also called temple blocks.

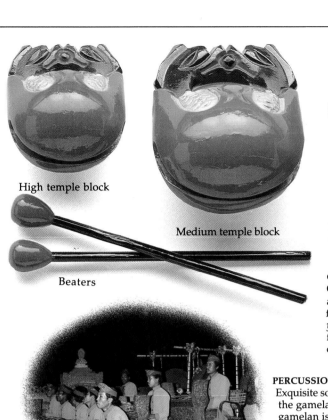

PERCUSSION ORCHESTRA
Exquisite sound is produced by the gamelans of Indonesia. A gamelan is an orchestra composed mainly of percussion instruments, each requiring great skill. It contains sets of gongs and metallophones, which are like xylophones but have bronze bars set in ornate frames.

TONGUE TWISTER
Many instruments of South and Central America originated in Africa. This *sansa*, or thumb piano, proves the link. It is played by twanging the metal tongues with the thumbs; the different lengths give different notes. The boat-shaped body and carved head are typically West African, but this instrument comes from the upper reaches of the Amazon.

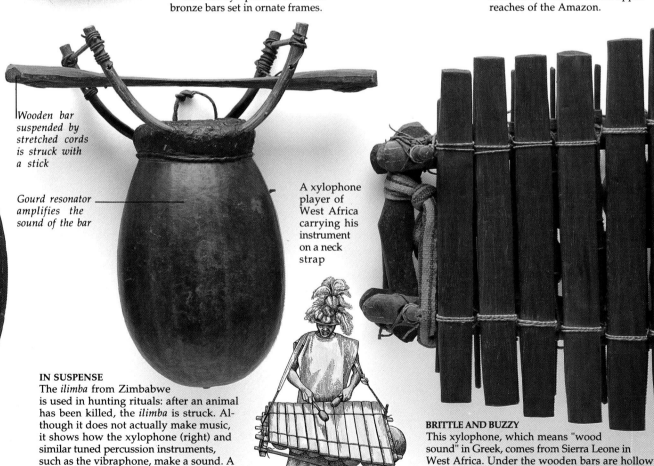

Wooden bar suspended by stretched cords is struck with a stick

Gourd resonator amplifies the sound of the bar

A xylophone player of West Africa carrying his instrument on a neck strap

Disk of elaborately worked bronze

IN SUSPENSE
The *ilimba* from Zimbabwe is used in hunting rituals: after an animal has been killed, the *ilimba* is struck. Although it does not actually make music, it shows how the xylophone (right) and similar tuned percussion instruments, such as the vibraphone, make a sound. A wooden bar is suspended over an open chamber or tube. Hitting the bar makes it vibrate, and the vibrations set the air in the chamber resonating with a hollow tone that amplifies the sound.

BRITTLE AND BUZZY
This xylophone, which means "wood sound" in Greek, comes from Sierra Leone in West Africa. Under the wooden bars are hollow gourds with small holes in the sides covered with membranes made from the egg cases of spiders. The membranes add a "buzz" to the sound of the xylophone.

55

Clang, crash, bang

NOISES PLAY an important part in many kinds of music: folk dancers often like to clap their hands in time to the music, for example, and many percussion instruments produce sounds that have no definite pitch or note. In much music, especially in South and Central America, musicians bang, shake, or scrape the kinds of instruments shown here. The lively rhythms of the sounds overlap to give a dancing beat that has terrific energy. Such "noises" can also be used to create moods. For instance, soft taps on a drum can sound menacing, while a drum roll is very dramatic.

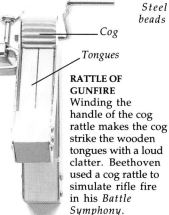

Cog

Tongues

RATTLE OF GUNFIRE
Winding the handle of the cog rattle makes the cog strike the wooden tongues with a loud clatter. Beethoven used a cog rattle to simulate rifle fire in his *Battle Symphony*.

Steel beads

RATTLE OF STEEL
The *cabaca* (pronounced "cabassa") is a South American rattle with steel beads strung on the outside.

SEEDS AND BEADS
Maracas are pairs of rattles that come from South America. They are traditionally made of hollow gourds containing loose seeds, but can also be made of wood and filled with beads. Both hands are normally used to shake them.

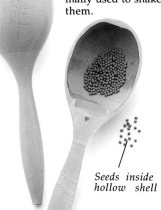

Seeds inside hollow shell

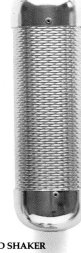

HAND SHAKER
Many percussion players in bands use shakers, which are hollow tubes containing loose beads (similar to maracas) and shaken in a lively rhythm. A small shaker can be gripped between the fingers while playing another instrument.

Police whistle

Train whistle

LITTLE BLOW-PEEP
A percussion player can blow short, shrieking blasts on a whistle to emphasize a rhythm while his hands are busy playing another instrument. Whistles also give sound effects: for example, the three-note whistle (right) sounds like a train whistle.

CUBAN CONCUSSION
These short wooden sticks are called claves or concussion sticks, and they come from Cuba. The two sticks are banged together to give a sharp crack. Although this may sound easy, the timing of a rhythm has to be exactly right.

One stick is held with the hand cupped so the sound resonates

Jingle mounted in slot in frame

DROPPING A CLANGER.
The tambourine is a small drum with jingles set into the frame. It is often decorated with ribbons, and can be held and played while dancing. The dancer taps the tambourine with the fingers and shakes it or bangs it against the body. Another possible effect is a roll made by sliding a wet thumb around the rim. In his ballet *Petrushka*, Igor Stravinsky directs the percussionist to drop a tambourine on the floor!

Pressing the top of each clapper sounds the castanets

HAND CLAPPERS
Castànets are wooden clappers held in the hands. Orchestral players may use the castanet machine (above).

A pair of castanets is held together by a cord

Flamenco dancer with castanets

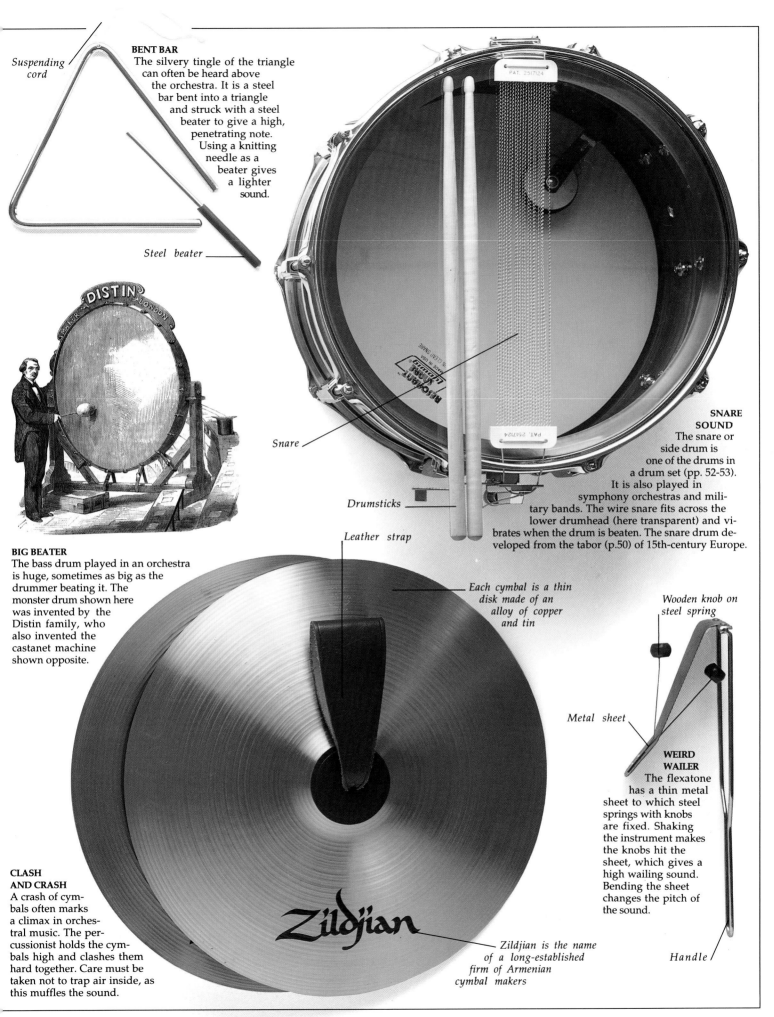

BENT BAR
The silvery tingle of the triangle can often be heard above the orchestra. It is a steel bar bent into a triangle and struck with a steel beater to give a high, penetrating note. Using a knitting needle as a beater gives a lighter sound.

Suspending cord

Steel beater

BIG BEATER
The bass drum played in an orchestra is huge, sometimes as big as the drummer beating it. The monster drum shown here was invented by the Distin family, who also invented the castanet machine shown opposite.

Snare

Drumsticks

Leather strap

SNARE SOUND
The snare or side drum is one of the drums in a drum set (pp. 52-53). It is also played in symphony orchestras and military bands. The wire snare fits across the lower drumhead (here transparent) and vibrates when the drum is beaten. The snare drum developed from the tabor (p.50) of 15th-century Europe.

Each cymbal is a thin disk made of an alloy of copper and tin

Wooden knob on steel spring

Metal sheet

WEIRD WAILER
The flexatone has a thin metal sheet to which steel springs with knobs are fixed. Shaking the instrument makes the knobs hit the sheet, which gives a high wailing sound. Bending the sheet changes the pitch of the sound.

CLASH AND CRASH
A crash of cymbals often marks a climax in orchestral music. The percussionist holds the cymbals high and clashes them hard together. Care must be taken not to trap air inside, as this muffles the sound.

Zildjian is the name of a long-established firm of Armenian cymbal makers

Handle

Electrifying music

ELECTRICITY FIRST BEGAN TO PLAY A PART IN MUSIC with the beginning of radio broadcasting early in the 20th century. Three elements are combined in order to make music louder: a microphone or "pick-up" converts sound waves into electrical signals. These are then strengthened by an amplifier and passed to a loudspeaker - basically a glorified telephone earpiece - which changes the signals back into sound waves. This system can boost the quietest of noises, and electrified sound has a character all its own. The electric guitar was invented to overcome the limited volume of the acoustic guitar and now dominates popular music.

Screw to attach strap

Pickup sockets

Solid wood body

Bridge socket

PIONEER GUITAR
The electric guitar is shown here before it was stripped down. It is a copy of the famous Fender Stratocaster, popularly known as the Strat. The pioneering Strat first made music in 1954, and has changed little since then. It introduced the double cutaway body, which made it easier to play, the tremolo arm to bend the notes, and the use of three pickups to vary the sound.

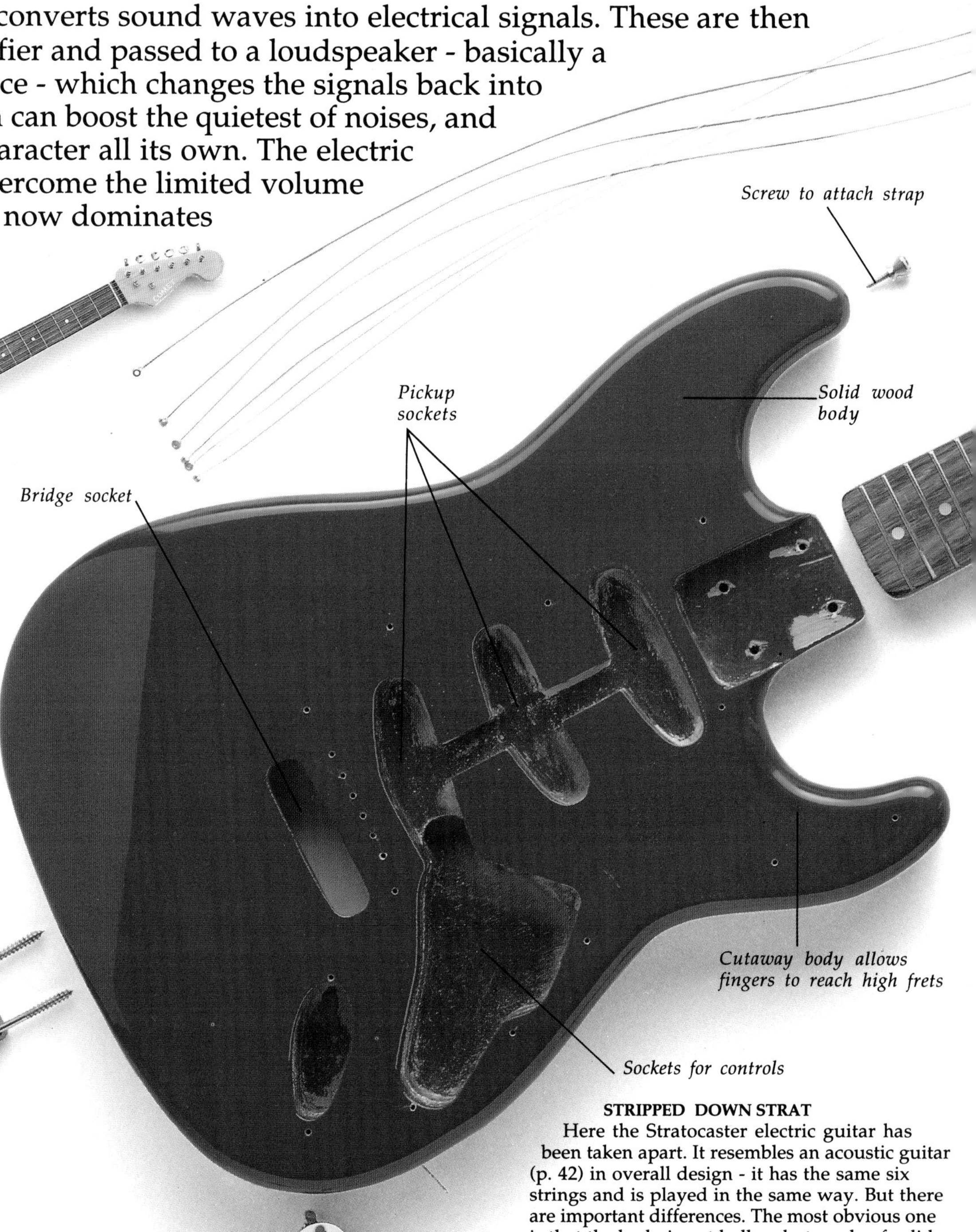

Cutaway body allows fingers to reach high frets

Strings fit into bridge

Sockets for controls

STRIPPED DOWN STRAT
Here the Stratocaster electric guitar has been taken apart. It resembles an acoustic guitar (p. 42) in overall design - it has the same six strings and is played in the same way. But there are important differences. The most obvious one is that the body is not hollow but made of solid wood painted red. Without its amplifier, an electric guitar makes little sound. Although the body can affect the sustaining quality of the notes, its main purpose is to provide a stable platform for the bridge that holds the strings and the pickups mounted beneath them. The pickups convert the vibrations of the strings into an electrical signal. This signal passes to the volume and tone controls before leaving the guitar at the output socket. A cable leads the signal to an amplifier, which has more controls, and finally to the loudspeaker.

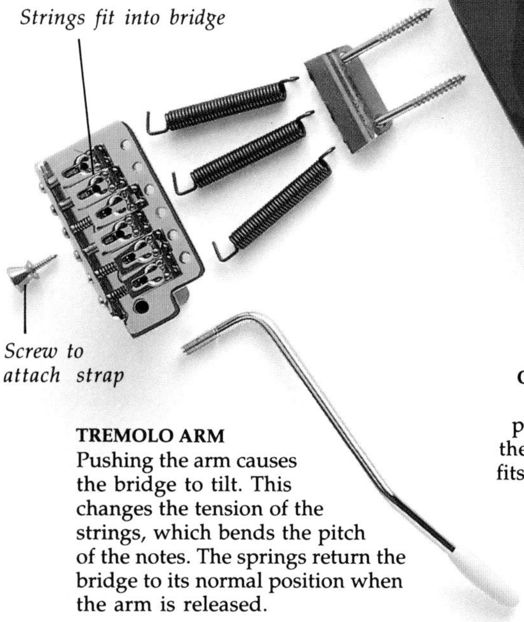

Screw to attach strap

OUTPUT SOCKET
A standard jack plug on the end of the amplifier lead fits into the socket.

TREMOLO ARM
Pushing the arm causes the bridge to tilt. This changes the tension of the strings, which bends the pitch of the notes. The springs return the bridge to its normal position when the arm is released.

Jack plug

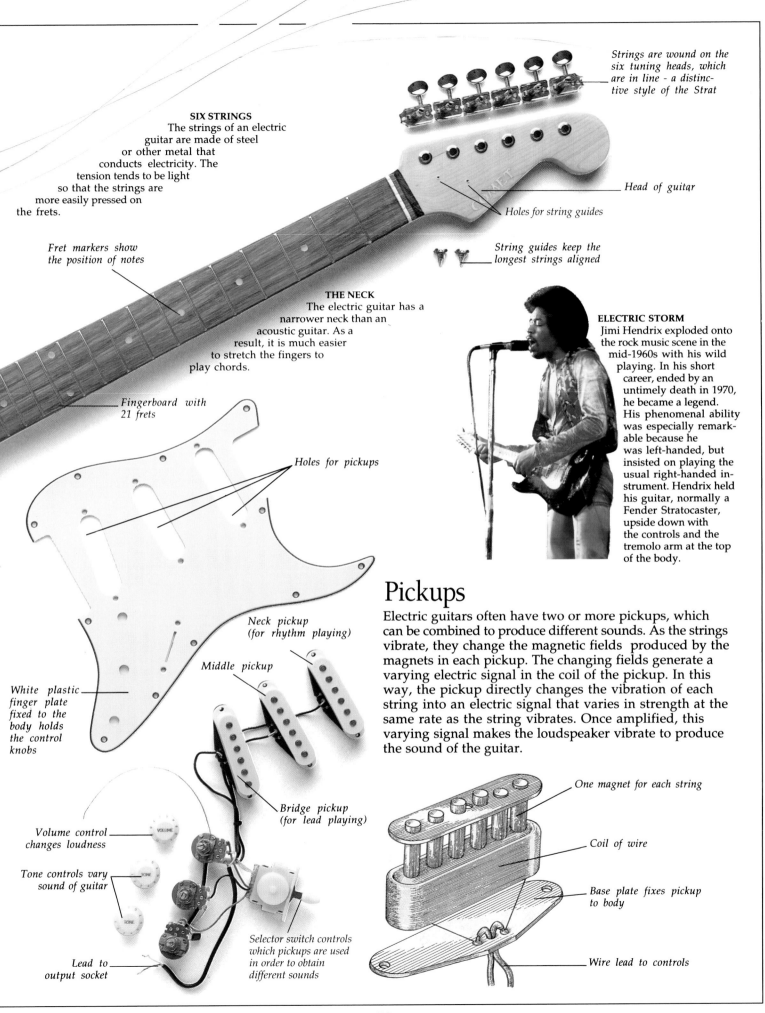

SIX STRINGS
The strings of an electric guitar are made of steel or other metal that conducts electricity. The tension tends to be light so that the strings are more easily pressed on the frets.

Strings are wound on the six tuning heads, which are in line - a distinctive style of the Strat

Head of guitar

Holes for string guides

Fret markers show the position of notes

String guides keep the longest strings aligned

THE NECK
The electric guitar has a narrower neck than an acoustic guitar. As a result, it is much easier to stretch the fingers to play chords.

ELECTRIC STORM
Jimi Hendrix exploded onto the rock music scene in the mid-1960s with his wild playing. In his short career, ended by an untimely death in 1970, he became a legend. His phenomenal ability was especially remarkable because he was left-handed, but insisted on playing the usual right-handed instrument. Hendrix held his guitar, normally a Fender Stratocaster, upside down with the controls and the tremolo arm at the top of the body.

Fingerboard with 21 frets

Holes for pickups

Pickups

Electric guitars often have two or more pickups, which can be combined to produce different sounds. As the strings vibrate, they change the magnetic fields produced by the magnets in each pickup. The changing fields generate a varying electric signal in the coil of the pickup. In this way, the pickup directly changes the vibration of each string into an electric signal that varies in strength at the same rate as the string vibrates. Once amplified, this varying signal makes the loudspeaker vibrate to produce the sound of the guitar.

Neck pickup (for rhythm playing)

Middle pickup

White plastic finger plate fixed to the body holds the control knobs

One magnet for each string

Coil of wire

Volume control changes loudness

Bridge pickup (for lead playing)

Tone controls vary sound of guitar

Base plate fixes pickup to body

Lead to output socket

Selector switch controls which pickups are used in order to obtain different sounds

Wire lead to controls

Rock guitars

THE ELECTRIC GUITAR gives rock music its sound. Most bands have two - often three - electric guitars. These are: a lead guitar that plays the solos, a rhythm guitar to play rocking rhythms behind the lead and the singer (often the same person), and a bass guitar that pumps out a driving bass line to urge the band forward. Add the power of the drum set (pp. 52-53) to all this electricity, and you have rock music in all its various forms. Because the solid body of an electric guitar does not produce the actual sound that is heard, it can be made in any shape that can be held. Rock guitars can come in a bizarre range of shapes, colors, and materials, but most stars put music first and prefer the more standard styles.

In this early model the strings pass through the back of the body

V FORMATION
The Gibson company pioneered the electric guitar, introducing the first one in 1935. This was basically a Spanish model fitted with a pick-up, and was called the Electric Spanish. In 1957 Gibson brought out the humbucker pickup, which has two coils to prevent hum. The famous Gibson Flying V guitar dates from 1958, when the company brought it out to revive its flagging fortunes. The futuristic style of the body was successful even though it was awkward to hold while playing. This particular instrument is an early 1958 Flying V, and it is now a collector's piece.

Twin humbucker pickups give fat sound characteristic of Gibson guitars

Solid wooden V-shaped body

Output socket

Bigsby tremolo arm

BEATLE MANIA
The Beatles were the most successful rock group of the 1960s. They had the classic rock line-up of two electric guitars (George Harrison on lead guitar and John Lennon on rhythm guitar - see above), bass guitar (Paul McCartney), and drums (Ringo Starr).

NOT SO SOLID ROCK
Not all electric guitars have solid bodies. Many are semi-acoustic guitars that have hollow bodies with f-shaped soundholes, like those in the violin (p. 32). The Gretsch 6120 semi-acoustic guitar was made famous by Eddie Cochran. This particular guitar dates from 1957 and bears the name of country music star Chet Atkins on the finger plate. It has a Bigsby tremolo arm, an alternative design to the Fender arm introduced on the Stratocaster guitar (p. 58).

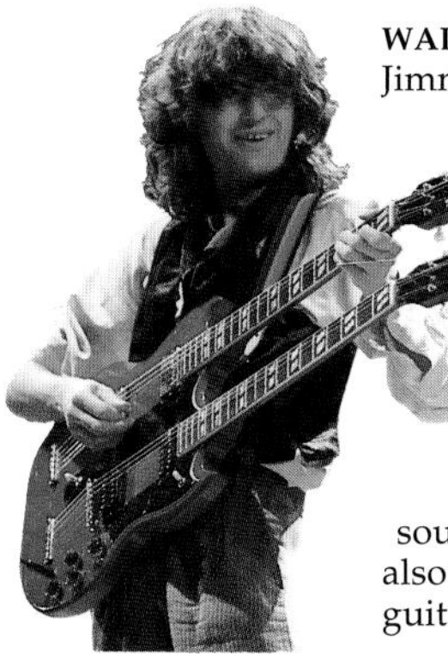

WALL OF SOUND
Jimmy Page, who founded the famous group Led Zeppelin in 1968, is known for the powerful "wall" of guitar sound that inspired the "heavy metal" style of rock music. He pioneered the use of a bow on the electric guitar, creating extraordinary sounds on the instrument, and also played double-headed guitars, as seen here.

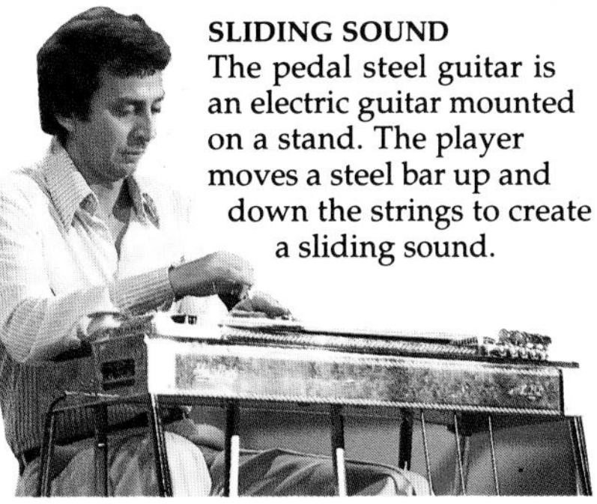

SLIDING SOUND
The pedal steel guitar is an electric guitar mounted on a stand. The player moves a steel bar up and down the strings to create a sliding sound.

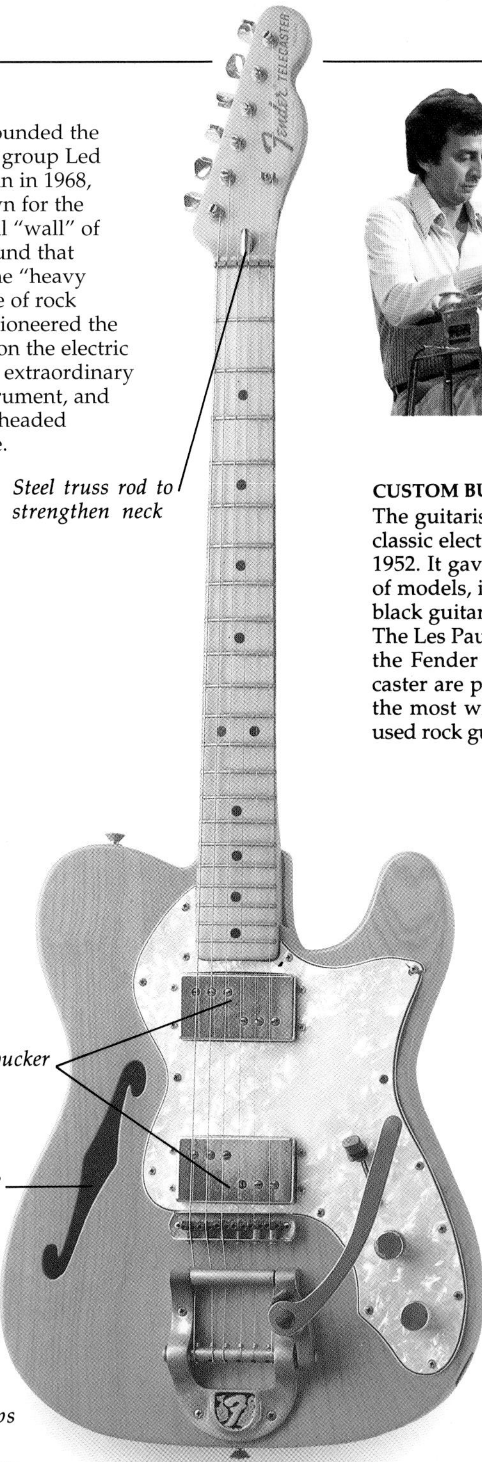

Steel truss rod to strengthen neck

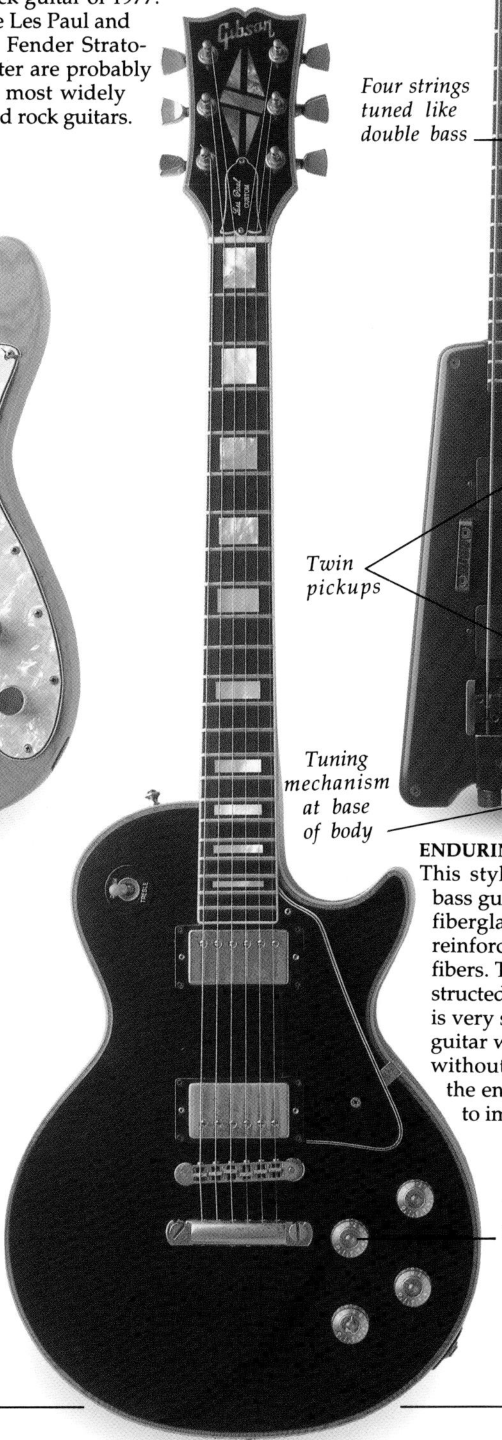

CUSTOM BUILT
The guitarist Les Paul designed a classic electric guitar for Gibson in 1952. It gave rise to a whole series of models, including this elegant black guitar of 1977. The Les Paul and the Fender Stratocaster are probably the most widely used rock guitars.

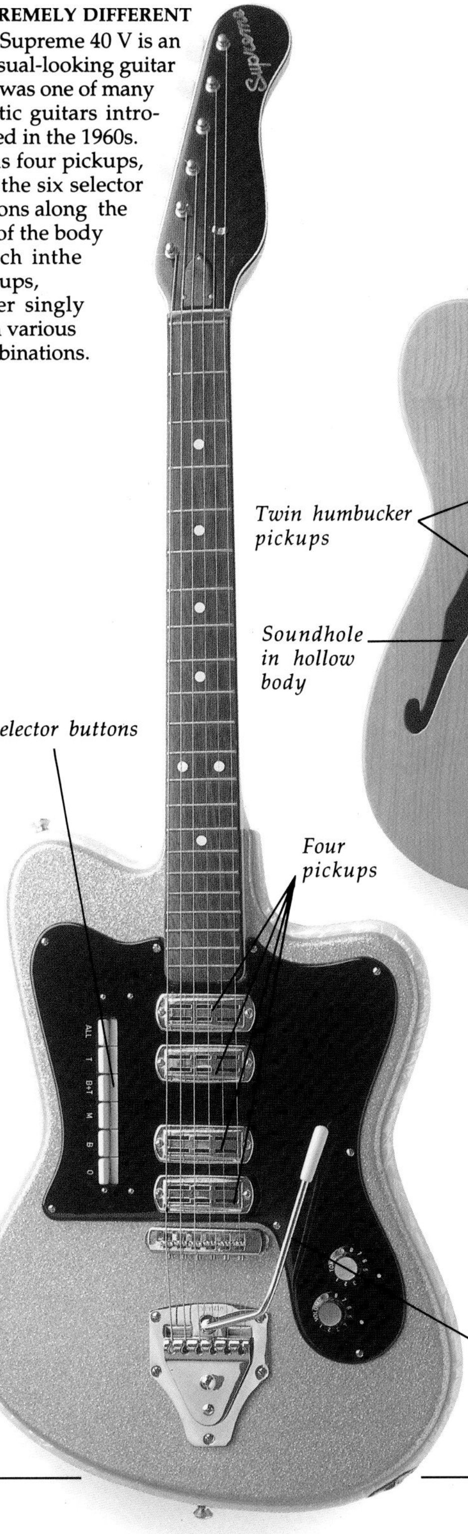

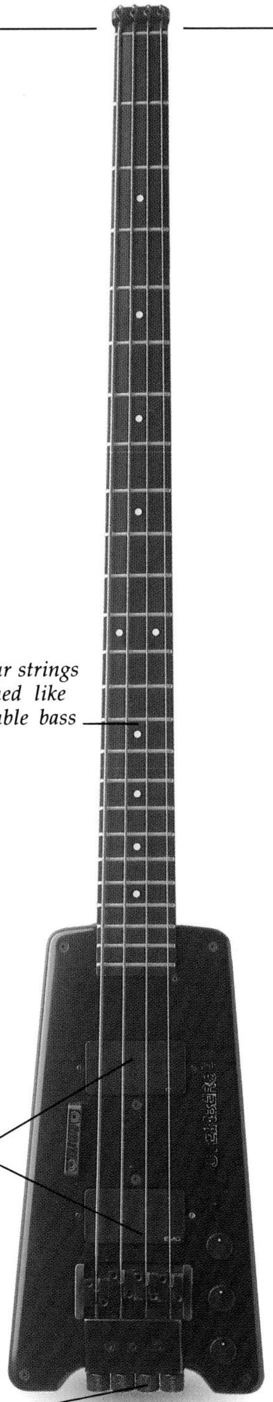

SUPREMELY DIFFERENT
The Supreme 40 V is an unusual-looking guitar and was one of many plastic guitars introduced in the 1960s. It has four pickups, and the six selector buttons along the top of the body switch inthe pickups, either singly or in various combinations.

Four strings tuned like double bass

Twin humbucker pickups

Soundhole in hollow body

Twin pickups

Selector buttons

Four pickups

Tuning mechanism at base of body

ENDURING SOUND
This stylish Steinberger bass guitar is made of fiberglass and plastic, reinforced with carbon fibers. The body is constructed in one piece and is very strong. The guitar was designed without a head at the end of the neck to improve the sound.

A PEDIGREE FENDER
Leo Fender built the first solid-body electric guitar in 1944. He then went on to found the Fender company, which produced the famous Stratocaster in 1954. Fender's first model was the Broadcaster of 1948, which was renamed the Telecaster. Shown here is the semi-acoustic Thinline Telecaster dating from 1973.

Volume and tone controls

Tremolo arm

Machine music

THE MUSIC OF THE FUTURE may well consist of sounds made by machines. The synthesizers and other electronic instruments shown here do not make their own sound; they produce an electric sound signal that goes along a cable to an amplifier and loudspeaker - like an electric guitar (pp. 58-59). These machines can make many different kinds of sound signals, giving a wide range of sounds. They can imitate other instruments or conjure up entirely new sounds. The computer is important in electronic music because it can control music-making machines and even create the music that they make.

Pad contains electronic components under the surface

ONE-MAN BAND
Popular music makes great use of electronic sounds. One of the pioneers is the French musician Jean-Michel Jarre. He was one of the first musicians to create an electronic orchestra in which he performed all the music himself.

PADS FOR DRUMS
Drummers can become electronic musicians with a kit of drum pads. Hitting the pad with a stick makes the pad produce an electronic sound signal that gives an electronic drum sound.

Standard drumstick

COMPUTER CONTROL
An ordinary home computer can be linked to electronic instruments like those shown here. Music applications let the computer store, process, and create musical notes. It can be turned into a recording studio; it can correct wrong and mistimed notes, and loop sequences. A modern advance is the soft synth, which is a virtual machine. Samples are stored inside the computer with virtually unlimited memory. Tapes are now almost obsolete in the small recording studio.

Floppy disks used in conjunction with keyboards for storing Midi sequences and small sounds

MIDI-Track ST

ELECTRONIC KEYBOARD
This synthesizer is played like a piano or organ. It can produce all kinds of realistic and unusual sounds by operating the controls above the keys. The display shows which sounds have been chosen. Keyboards can also be stand-alone workstations which can sequence, process, and store music like a computer.

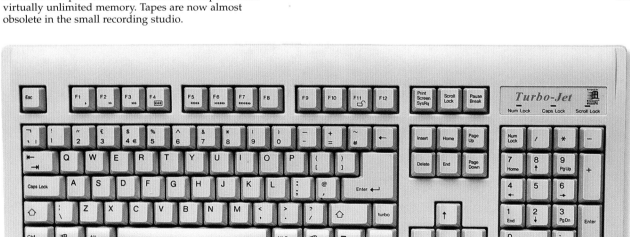

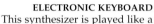

Standard keyboard

Number keys

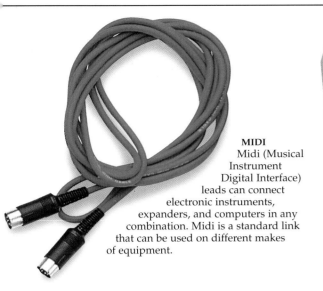

MIDI
Midi (Musical Instrument Digital Interface) leads can connect electronic instruments, expanders, and computers in any combination. Midi is a standard link that can be used on different makes of equipment.

EXPANDER
This black box contains 160 sounds. It connects to an electronic instrument or computer. Playing the instrument makes sounds come out from it, expanding the instrument's sound range. Sample CDs can also produce new libraries of sound.

SAMPLER-SYNTH
Modern samplers (like this below) have radically changed and improved the quality of sound produced. They have unlimited storage, polyphony (playing up to 128 "voices" or notes at the same time), and are multi-timbral (able to play up to 32 separate instruments at once).

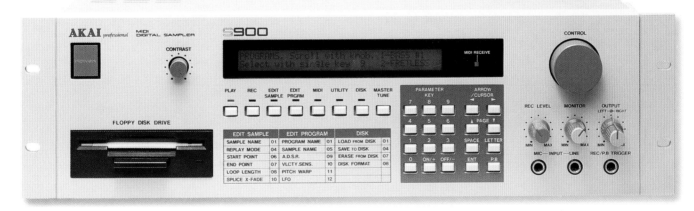

Did you know?

FASCINATING FACTS

❖ Secular music during the Middle Ages was often performed by wandering troubadours who accompanied themselves on the lute or the harp. The songs they sang were mostly narrative ballads on the themes of heroic adventures or affairs of the heart.

❖ In medieval times, one of the most familiar musical instruments was the hornpipe, which resembled a recorder with a hollowed-out cow's horn strapped to the end.

Hornpipe

❖ During the 16th and 17th centuries, the early guitar was much less popular than the vehuela, a closely related 12-stringed instrument. As the guitar evolved toward its present form, however, it came to dominate the field and render its rival obsolete.

❖ Johann Sebastian Bach had two wives and 20 children. Two of his sons—the eldest, Wilhelm Friedemann, and the youngest, Johann Christian—became successful composers in their own right.

Portrait of George Frederick Handel by Sir James Thornhill

❖ Both George Frederick Handel and Robert Schumann studied law for some time before they turned to music as a full-time career, while Alexander Borodin was originally a medical chemist and Nikolai Rimsky-Korsakov trained to be an officer in the navy.

❖ G.F. Handel and J. S. Bach both went blind toward the end of their lives; Ludwig van Beethoven began to lose his hearing when he was about 30, and by his early fifties, he was totally deaf.

❖ An extravagant romantic in emotional as well as musical terms, Beethoven often fell in love—sometimes with his aristocratic pupils— yet he never married.

❖ Franz Schubert lived an extravagantly creative and frequently poverty-stricken bohemian life in early 19th century Vienna. He died of syphilis when he was only 31.

❖ From an early age, Robert Schumann was emotionally unstable. Originally trained as a pianist, he had to abandon his career when obsessive practice damaged his fingers. Later, he tried to drown himself in the Rhine River, and he spent the last two years of his life in total darkness in a psychiatric hospital.

❖ In contrast, Felix Mendelssohn's life was one of remarkable success and happiness. Extremely talented as a conductor and pianist as well as a composer, he was also charming, handsome, and extremely rich, having inherited a fortune from his father. Mendolssohn's tragedy was his early death at the age of 39.

❖ Sickly with tuberculosis for much of his adult life, Frederic Chopin had a notorious liaison with the French writer Amandine Aurore Lucie Dupin, who scandalized society by dressing in men's clothes and assuming the pseudonym George Sand.

❖ A great virtuoso pianist as well as a composer, Franz Liszt was born in Hungary, and he based his popular *Hungarian Rhapsodies* on the gypsy music of his homeland. Liszt never spoke Hungarian, though. He spoke French.

❖ Richard Wagner composed one of the best-known tunes in the history of western music: the Wedding March from his opera *Lohengrin*, popularly known as "Here Comes the Bride." Wagner himself was married to Cosima von Bulow, daughter of Franz Liszt.

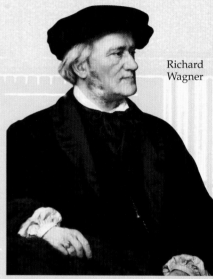

Richard Wagner

❖ Richard Strauss's *Also Sprach Zarathustra* (theme of the film *2001: A Space Odyssey*, and, unofficially, of the U.S. space program) created a furor at its 1896 premiere. At a time when inspiration usually came from poetry or nature, Strauss based this work on the writings of tortured philosopher Frederick Nietzsche.

❖ Facing financial ruin and emotional breakdown, Pyotr Tchaikovsky was rescued by a rich widow, Nadezhda von Meck. She agreed to provide him with a generous income on the condition that they never meet but communicate only by letter.

Franz Liszt playing in Vienna for the Austrian royal family

QUESTIONS AND ANSWERS

British conductor Simon Rattle

Q Where does the word "music" come from?

A Its root is the Greek word *mousiké*, which originally referred to all the arts presided over by the nine Muses, the goddesses of the arts in classical mythology. Daughters of Zeus and Mnemosyne (Memory), the Muses were first listed by the early Greek poet Hesiod, although their number, some of their names, and their associated arts sometimes vary. The word "museum" has the same origin as "music," and initially described a place connected with the Muses.

The facade of the Teátro Juarez in Guanajuato, Mexico, is crowned with statues of the Muses.

Q Where does the word "orchestra" come from?

A Again, from a Greek word that described the semicircular space where the actors and chorus performed in a traditional theater or auditorium. It was in 17th-century France, though, that the term orchestra was first used to describe the space where musicians sat in front of a stage, and later applied to the musicians themselves.

Q What's the difference between chamber music and the other musical forms that make up a concert?

A Even after public concerts became a popular part of European cultural life, there were certain pieces—those that could be played by a small number of players in a small room—that were heard only in the private salons of wealthy music lovers. This rarified repertoire was known as chamber music. It was not until the pop-star virtuosos Franz Liszt and Niccolo Paganini began to give solo recitals at the peak of their success in the mid-19th century that such small-scale pieces were heard by the concert-going public. (Previously, instrumentalists had always performed with a large orchestra.)

Q Have orchestras always had conductors in the way they do now?

A During the 17th and 18th centuries, the conductor was also one of the instrumentalists—harpsichord and violin were favorite instruments. By the 19th century, though, orchestras had grown dramatically in size and complexity, so they required the full attention of the person controlling them. Today, conductors not only beat time and direct loudness, they almost play the orchestra like an instrument, creating the style and expression of the music being performed. Many famous composers, such as Mahler and Stravinsky, were also conductors of note, and a number of famous conductors, such as Arturo Toscanini and Leonard Bernstein, achieved a level of celebrity equal to that of leading soloists.

Record Breakers

 EXTRAVAGANT OUTPUT
Few composers are as prolific as the 18th-century Italian Antonio Vivaldi: He produced more than 400 concertos, 23 symphonies, 75 sonatas, more than 40 operas, and a considerable body of sacred music.

 WONDERBOY
By the age of six, Wolfgang Amadeus Mozart was well known as a composer and pianist, undertaking wildly successful concert tours across Europe. In his early twenties, he was adored and admired by the entire musical world, yet he died in poverty when he was only 35.

 UNIVERSAL SOUND
The guitar is the most popular instrument in the modern world; versatile, portable, and enjoyable to play even with limited skill, it has a distinctive sound that is part of the musical culture of almost every country on earth.

 PUBLIC APPEAL
The first public concerts were held in Leipzig, Germany, in 1743. Before this time, operas and musical events were staged only for select audiences, at royal courts and in the grand houses of the aristocracy.

Guitar

Who's who?

THE MUSIC WE HEAR at concerts, on the radio, and in recordings is part of a tradition that reaches back hundreds of years to the church and the royal courts of the Middle Ages. Over time, music has developed through recognized periods, from the Baroque style, through the Classical age of Mozart and Beethoven, to the Romantic era in the 19th century. Modern music has branched out into a number of different strands: It can be tuneful and structured, harsh and electronic, or somewhere in between. Today, the concert repertoire includes pieces from all these traditions, and learning a little about the major composers involved can enhance your enjoyment and understanding of their music considerably. Composers are listed by birth date.

Medieval troubadour

- **CLAUDIO MONTEVERDI**
1567–1643 ITALIAN
One of the first Baroque composers, Monteverdi is best known for his madrigals (songs for several voices), operas (like *The Coronation of Poppea*), and sacred music. His work displayed new styles of harmony and melody that helped define the period.

- **ANTONIO VIVALDI**
1678–1741 ITALIAN
Violinist and outstanding Baroque composer, Vivaldi was an important figure in the development of the solo concerto. His music, which includes the massively popular *Four Seasons*, was widely neglected until the 1930s.

Antonio Vivaldi

- **JOHANN SEBASTIAN BACH**
1685–1750 GERMAN
Representing the height of the Baroque era, Bach was described by Wagner as "the most stupendous miracle in all music." Among his celebrated works are the *St. Matthew Passion* and *St. John Passion*, the *Brandenburg Concertos*, and the collection of preludes and fugues known as *The Well-Tempered Clavier*.

- **GEORGE FREDERICK HANDEL**
1685–1759 GERMAN
Born in Germany, Handel resided for some time in Italy and also spent much of his life in England. A virtuoso on the organ and the harpsichord, he is known mainly as the composer of *Water Music*, *Music for the Royal Fireworks*, the *Messiah*, and *The Harmonious Blacksmith*, a set of harpsichord pieces.

- **JOSEPH HAYDN**
1732–1809 AUSTRIAN
First of the three giants of the Classical era (the others are Mozart and Beethoven, both of whom he taught), Haydn pioneered the symphonic form; he wrote more than 100 symphonies, plus various string quartets and the oratorios *The Creation* and *The Seasons*.

- **WOLFGANG AMADEUS MOZART**
1756–1791 AUSTRIAN
A towering figure in musical history, Mozart is perhaps the most versatile of all composers: He created some of the greatest operas ever written (such as *The Marriage of Figaro* and *Don Giovanni*), plus an enormous body of orchestral music unique in its melodic richness and purity.

- **LUDWIG VAN BEETHOVEN**
1770–1827 GERMAN
Based in the Classical tradition, Beethoven forms a strong link with Romanticism. His legacy includes nine symphonies—the third (*Eroica*), the fifth, the sixth (*Pastoral*), and the ninth (*Choral*) being the most famous—32 piano sonatas (including the *Moonlight* and the *Appassionata*) and one opera, *Fidelio*.

Ludwig van Beethoven

- **FRANZ SCHUBERT**
1797–1828 AUSTRIAN
Although he died at 31, Schubert wrote eight symphonies, more than 600 songs, 17 overtures, masses, and choral works, and an outstanding collection of piano pieces. A major Romantic figure, he is the heir to Mozart and Beethoven in the warmth and flow of his music.

- **HECTOR BERLIOZ**
1803–1869 FRENCH
Berlioz's significance lies in his pioneering of program music and in the exciting ways he used the orchestra in the process. Notable works are the *Symphonie Fantastique* and the operas *Les Troyens* and *Benvenuto Cellini*.

- **FELIX MENDELSSOHN**
1809–1847 GERMAN
A Romantic influenced by Classicism, Mendelssohn produced a number of well-loved concert classics such as the *Fingal's Cave* and *A Midsummer Night's Dream* overtures, the *Italian* and *Scottish Symphonies*, and *Songs Without Words* for the piano.

- **FREDERIC CHOPIN**
1810–1849 POLISH
Chopin was a brilliant pianist, and his creative output, which includes many very familiar waltzes, sonatas, and preludes, is almost exclusively for this instrument. His deeply felt (and very Romantic) nationalism shows in his polonaises and mazurkas and in the *Revolutionary Etude*, inspired by the 1831 Russian capture of Warsaw.

Frederic Chopin

- **ROBERT SCHUMANN**
1810–1856 GERMAN
Another leading light of Romanticism, Schumann is known chiefly for his piano music (much of which was interpreted by his wife, Clara, a noted virtuosa), and for his songs, many inspired by Romantic poems. Uniquely for the time, Schumann was also a writer and critic who championed Berlioz, Chopin, and Brahms.

• FRANZ LISZT
1811–1886 HUNGARIAN

In his day, Liszt was valued more as a pianist and teacher than a composer. Another champion of program music, he believed inspiration should be unrestricted by form and produced popular works such as *Liebesträume* and the *Hungarian Dances*, which anticipated Impressionism.

• RICHARD WAGNER
1813–1883 GERMAN

Although his output is largely operatic (he wrote the Ring Cycle, *Lohengrin*, and *Parsifal*), Wagner's influence is enormous. His melodic line, dramatic harmony, and unique instrumentation represent the peak of Romanticism and point toward the developments of the 20th century.

Richard Wagner

• ANTON BRUCKNER
1824–1896 AUSTRIAN

A Wagner disciple, Bruckner composed 11 symphonies and seven masses. With its enormous scope, elaborate themes, and complex developments, his work carries Wagner's influence firmly into the sphere of orchestral music.

• JOHANNES BRAHMS
1833–1897 GERMAN

Essentially Romantic, Brahms's music reveals Classical influences. Brahms and the pure Romantics Wagner and Bruckner were great rivals, but both sides influenced 20th-century music strongly. His output includes symphonies, songs, concertos, and one of the most familiar lullabies ever written.

• PYOTR ILYICH TCHAIKOVSKY
1840–1893 RUSSIAN

Creator of countless well-loved tunes, Tchaikovsky popularized Russian music in the late 19th century. An energetic composer who wrote symphonies, operas, concertos, overtures, and songs, he is remembered chiefly for his melodic ballets *Swan Lake*, *Sleeping Beauty*, and *The Nutcracker*.

• ANTONIN DVORAK
1841–1904 CZECH

With a style best described (like that of Brahms) as Classical-Romantic, Dvořák is closely associated with Czech nationalism, and it was his *Slavonic Dances* that first gained wide success. The hugely popular *Symphony No. 9: From the New World*, however (written in New York), is most closely linked with him.

• EDVARD GRIEG
1843–1907 NORWEGIAN

Another strongly nationalistic composer, Grieg was the first to bring Scandinavian music to world notice. Romantic in inclination, he was influenced by Norwegian folk melodies, which appear repeatedly in his best-known pieces—the *Piano Concerto* and the incidental music for Ibsen's play *Peer Gynt*.

• EDWARD ELGAR
1857–1934 ENGLISH

Largely self taught, Elgar did not achieve real success until the publication of *Enigma Variations*, when he was over 40 years old. Once established, he carried the Romantic flame into the 20th century with his orchestral and chamber music and choral work.

• GUSTAV MAHLER
1860–1911 CZECH

Mahler's music is rich and lyrical in the Romantic-Classical style, yet powerfully individual. He was thought of as a conductor during his life, however, and his genius was not appreciated until long after he died. His work includes nine symphonies and a series of vocal pieces, including *The Song of the Earth*.

• CLAUDE DEBUSSY
1862–1918 FRENCH

Often labeled the first modern composer, Debussy is closely associated with musical Impressionism. His well-known works include *Prélude à l'après-midi d'un faune* and *La Mer*.

Claude Debussy

• RICHARD STRAUSS
1864–1949 GERMAN

Rooted in Romanticism, Strauss created new, influential styles of orchestration and harmony. He worked mainly in orchestral music and opera, his tone poems *Don Juan* and *Also Sprach Zarathustra* and his opera *Der Rosenkavalier* being particularly familiar.

• JEAN SIBELIUS
1865–1957 FINNISH

A nationalist who, like Grieg, drew on folk melodies, Sibelius wrote seven monumental symphonies. Two shorter works, *The Swan of Tuonela* and *Finlandia*, are popular favorites.

• SERGE RACHMANINOV
1873–1943 RUSSIAN

The emotionality of Rachmaninov's music combines Romanticism with folk influences. Particularly well loved are the *Rhapsody on a Theme of Paganini* and the *Second Piano Concerto*, used memorably in the movies *Brief Encounter* and *Shine*.

• ARNOLD SCHOENBERG
1874–1951 AUSTRIAN

An influential modernist, Schoenberg began by producing lush melodies but later turned to atonality. Finding this lacked cohesion, he invented a new system: the 12-note or Serial system, which was refined further by Anton Weber and Alban Berg.

Maurice Ravel

• MAURICE RAVEL
1875–1937 FRENCH

Known, like Debussy, as an Impressionist, Ravel produced music that was substantial and finely crafted. Many of his pieces have become concert favorites, including *La Valse*, *Boléro*, and the ballet *Daphnis et Chloe*.

• IGOR STRAVINSKY
1882–1971 RUSSIAN

Also vastly influential, Stravinsky reflects traditional forms in his work, but its striking aspect—and his main contribution to modernism—is his use of rhythm. Much of his music (including *The Firebird*, *Petrushka*, *Pulcinella*, and the rhythmically revolutionary *The Rite of Spring*) was commissioned for the Ballet Russe, but he also wrote orchestral and choral pieces and operas, including *The Rake's Progress* and *Oedipus Rex*.

• SERGEI PROKOFIEV
1891–1953 RUSSIAN

Although at one time a member of the Soviet avant-garde (early progressive work includes his *Symphony No. 2* and opera *The Love for Three Oranges*), Prokofiev retained his integrity and his individuality while complying with state pressure to compose in a more populist style. Particularly familiar are his narrated children's piece *Peter and the Wolf* and the supremely lyrical ballet *Romeo and Juliet*.

Dmitri Shostakovich

• DMITRI SHOSTAKOVICH
1906–1975 RUSSIAN

Like Prokofiev, Shostakovich was a modernist in Soviet Russia. He wrote several operas and ballets and orchestral music that includes 15 symphonies. The *Fifth*, *Seventh* (*Leningrad*), *Eighth*, and *Tenth* symphonies, and a few of his concertos are performed regularly.

• THE MODERN AGE

Today's diverse and unorthodox music has its origins in the work of Pierre Boulez (French), Luigi Nono (Italian), and Karlheinz Stockhausen (German), who began to explore electronics in the mid-20th century. At its most extreme, this modernism takes in the work of John Cage, who makes startling sounds with buzzers and cans; his 4'33" consists only of silence and background noise. As the new century begins, there seem to be as many compositional styles and forms to be explored as there are individual composers.

Find out more

PEOPLE WHO LOVE MUSIC often find themselves drawn to it in lots of different ways: listening to CDs and tapes, going to live performances, studying music history, and—most rewarding of all—creating it themselves. Certainly, mastering a solo instrument, joining a local band or orchestra, or just getting a few friends together to experiment with sounds can enrich both your feeling for music and the pleasure it brings you. Another way to increase your involvement is by joining a youth music group, volunteering at a concert hall, or visiting a recording or mixing studio. If your interest is in classical music, take advantage of any facilities offered by your nearest symphony orchestra, such as special classes or performances. For a more intensive experience, explore the resources offered by a music camp, where expert instruction and opportunities for performance are combined with the chance to meet new people from around the world.

YOUTH AND MUSIC
Rehearsing together and playing in front of an audience teaches music students how the sounds made by different instruments blend and contrast to create a finished performance. Here, composer and conductor John Williams works with the UCLA Youth Orchestra.

PLAYING AT SCHOOL
Many secondary schools that offer music as part of a general curriculum have their own student orchestra and band.

LEADING STRINGS
Playing in an orchestra's string section (violins, violas, cellos, and basses) often involves carrying the main melody of the piece being performed.

MUSIC LESSONS

As well as giving individual lessons, music teachers can often provide students with their first experience of playing with others—a valuable step between producing sound by themselves and becoming part of an orchestra.

USEFUL WEB SITES

- General classical music Web site including historical and biographical notes (with soundbite samples) and glossary: **/w3.rz-berlin.mpg.de/cmp/classmus.html**
- The Mozart Project, a comprehensive site covering the life, times, and music of Wolfgang Amadeus Mozart: **www.mozartproject.org**
- Dedicated George Frederick Handel Web site with links for concerts, workshops, festivals, societies, and general information relating to Handel: **www.gfhandel.org**
- Web site of the American Classical Music Hall of Fame and Museum: **www.classicalhall.org**
- Web site of the Country Music Hall of Fame and Museum: **www.halloffame.org**
- Web site of the Rock and Roll Hall of Fame and Museum: **www.rockhall.com**

George Frederick Handel

GEORGE FREDERICK HANDEL Esqr
born February XXIII MDCLXXXIV.
died April XIV MDCCLIX   L.F.Roubiliac invt et

ROCK AND ROLL HALL OF FAME

The Rock and Roll Hall of Fame and Museum was designed by Chinese-American architect I.M. Pei. Intended to "echo the energy of rock and roll," it is set on a huge plaza that acts as a meeting place for enthusiasts and an outdoor arena.

Tower rises straight up from the city's harbor.

Elevated exhibition space

Places to Visit

BLUE LAKE FINE ARTS CAMP, TWIN LAKE, MICHIGAN
Combining a music camp with an international exchange program, the Blue Lake facility arranges for young people from Europe, Asia, and North America to perform in one another's countries, learn with other instrumentalists, and stay in private homes abroad.
www.bluelake.org/internat

TANGLEWOOD MUSIC CENTER, LENOX, MASSACHUSETTS
On the grounds of a former Berkshires farm, this summer home of the Boston Symphany Orchestra hosts indoor and outdoor concerts and recitals throughout the summer. Visitors can picnic on the lawns as they listen.

WASBE INTERNATIONAL YOUTH CAMP SCHOLARSHIP PROGRAM
Run by a collection of participating music camps (some of whom offer scholarships), this program helps music students from places as diverse as Brazil, Norway, and China study in other countries.
www.wasbe.com/en/programs/youthcamp

CLASSICAL MUSIC HALL OF FAME AND MUSEUM, CINCINNATI, OHIO
Dedicated to those who have made a significant contribution to American classical music, the Hall of Fame also mounts exhibits designed to encourage new audiences to enjoy the repertoire it celebrates.

COUNTRY MUSIC HALL OF FAME AND MUSEUM, NASHVILLE, TENNESSEE
Based at the international heart of country music, Nashville, Tennessee, the Hall of Fame features live entertainment, interactive displays, digital film presentations, and a huge shop with an outstanding selection of music, collectibles, and clothing.

ROCK AND ROLL HALL OF FAME AND MUSEUM, CLEVELAND, OHIO
The permanent collection at this unique attraction includes items that relate to early blues figures as well as current pop idols. In addition to film, video, and music, there are instruments, scores, handwritten lyrics, costumes, props, and memorabilia spanning more than a century of popular music history.

HANDEL MUSEUM, LONDON, ENGLAND
Located in the central London house where George Frederick Handel wrote his *Messiah*, this museum includes exhibition space, re-creations of some of Handel's own rooms, a study center, and a collection of portraits—of Handel himself and of contemporaries such as John Gay and Alexander Pope.

Glossary

A carillon is played on large bells.

ACCENT Note or chord that is stressed or emphasized

ACCIDENTAL Symbol used to raise or lower the pitch of a note (*see also* PITCH)

ADAGIO In slow time; musical passage performed this way

ALLEGRO Fast moving, happy; musical passage performed this way. *Allegretto* means in fairly brisk time.

ANDANTE Walking pace, moderately slow; musical passage performed this way. *Andantino* means not too slow

ARPEGGIO In the manner of a harp; playing the notes of a chord one after the other rather than at the same time

ATONAL Music that is not written or performed in a particular key (*see also* KEY)

BAR Section marked on a musical staff to divide a composition into parts of equal time value

Gibson Les Paul electric guitar, 1956

The electric guitar plays a major role in both rock and blues music.

BLUES Expressive, melancholic, and rhythmic form of American music

CADENCE Close of a musical phrase; end of a sequence of chords. A *cadenza* is a virtuoso passage for a soloist near the end of a musical movement.

CAPRICCIO Lively, witty, and usually short composition

CARILLON Chime of bells, either rung from a church tower or created on a keyboard; tune played on bells

CHAMBER MUSIC Music intended to be played by a small orchestra in an intimate setting. A chamber orchestra is one with a limited number of players.

CHORD Group of notes combined according to a given system and usually sounded together

CHROMATIC The full scale, including all 12 notes a semitone apart within an octave (*see also* DIATONIC)

CLEF Sign placed at the beginning of a musical staff to indicate the register of the notes

CODA Concluding section, often elaborate and distinct, of a musical movement or piece of music

CONCERTO Musical composition, often in three movements, for one or more solo instruments and an orchestra

COUNTERPOINT Melody added as an independent—but linked and complementary—accompaniment to an existing melody

CRESCENDO Gradual increase of loudness, or progress toward a climax; musical passage performed this way. *Decrescendo* (or *diminuendo*) means gradual decrease of loudness.

DIATONIC The seven-note major and minor scale system (*see also* CHROMATIC)

DISSONANCE Incongruous combination of notes that form harsh or jarring chords (*see also* HARMONY)

DUET Composition for two musicians; group of two musicians

ELECTRONIC MUSIC Music that is produced or performed by electronics alone, without any pipes, strings, etc.

FANTASIE, FANTASIA Free musical form without rigid structure

FINALE Last movement of a composition; conclusion of a movement

FORTE Loud. *Fortissimo* means very loud, *triple forte* means as loud as possible, and *mezzoforte* means half-loud.

FUGUE Piece of music constructed on a single theme worked in two or more parts according to strict structural rules

GLISSANDO Drawing (or gliding) a finger rapidly up or down a succession of notes, especially on piano keys or harp strings

HARMONY Ordered combination of notes that form pleasing chords (*see also* DISSONANCE)

IMITATION Repetition of a main phrase by other parts

IMPROVISATION Process of writing music or playing an instrument ad lib; composing sounds as they are produced

INSTRUMENTATION Distribution of musical parts among the various instruments in an orchestra; scoring; orchestration

INTERVAL Difference of pitch between two notes

Celebrated jazz saxophonist Courtney Pine

JAZZ American music, often improvised, with characteristic harmonies and rhythms. Originated in the early 20th century, jazz has evolved from a number of folk and African-American styles.

KEY System of related notes predominating in a piece of music

LEGATO Smoothly, evenly, without breaks (opposite of STACCATO)

LENTO Slowly

MELODY Arrangement of notes in expressive succession

METER Division of beats into regular bars of simple or compound time

METRONOME Machine for marking time using a pendulum

MODULATION Transition from one key to another

MOTIF Smallest unit, or kernel, of a melody

NOCTURNE Slow, dreamy musical composition, often for piano

NOTATION Representation of musical details, such as pitch, duration, and so on, by symbols

OCTAVE Interval of eight notes between a given note and its higher or lower corresponding note

OCTET Composition for eight musicians; group of eight musicians

OVERTURE Orchestral introduction to a larger piece of music such as an opera. A concert overture is a symphonic piece with a single movement. (*see also* SYMPHONY)

PIANO Soft. *Pianissimo* means very soft, *pianissimo possible* means as soft as possible, and *mezzopiano* means half-soft.

PITCH The degree of highness or lowness of a sound

PRESTO Fast. *Prestissimo* means extremely fast.

QUARTET Composition for four musicians; group of four musicians

QUINTET Composition for five musicians; group of five musicians

REPRISE Repetition of a dominant musical passage

RHYTHM Aspect of music concerned with the pattern of accents and duration of notes

ROCK Style of popular music derived from blues, jazz, and country music during the 1950s (*see also* BLUES, JAZZ)

RONDO Musical composition with a dominant theme that returns repeatedly

RUBATO Expressive slowing then quickening of musical tempo

SCHERZO Lively, playful; musical passage performed this way. A *scherzino* is a small scherzo.

SCORE Copy showing all the parts of a musical composition

SEPTET Composition for seven musicians; group of seven musicians

Metronome

SEXTET Composition for six musicians; group of six musicians

SONATA Instrumental piece in three or four related movements, the first of which is highly developed and extended. Sonata form describes a composition in which two musical themes are set out, developed, and reinstated.

STACCATO Choppy, abrupt (opposite of LEGATO)

STAFF or **STAVE** Set of parallel lines on (or between) which musical annotation is positioned according to its pitch

SUITE Set of dances or instrumental compositions with related themes; collection of short pieces taken from a longer piece, such as *The Nutcracker Suite* from the ballet *The Nutcracker*

SYNCOPATION Displacement of accents from heavy to light; offbeat accentuation

SYMPHONY Musical composition in sonata form for full orchestra, usually in four movements (*see also* SONATA)

TEMPO Measure of time and rhythm

THEME Melody developed into variations

TONAL Music with the motivation and coherence provided by the conventional key system (*see also* KEY)

TONE Pitch, quality, and strength of musical sound

TRANSPOSE Translate to another key

TRIO Composition for three musicians; group of three musicians

VARIATION Melody repeated in a changed or elaborated form

VIBRATO Trembling; rapid, slight variation in pitch

Quartet

SURVEY OF MUSICAL STYLES

BAROQUE Defined by ornate and extravagant arrangements and melodies, Baroque style held sway in Europe from about 1600 to 1750. First applied in this context during the 19th century, the term comes from the Portuguese *barrocco*, meaning misshapen pearl; its use originally suggested something twisted or unnatural, but this is no longer true.

CLASSICISM A reaction against Baroque exuberance, the Classical era (around 1750 to 1820) was about balance, reason, and finish. Its name refers to the classicism of the ancient world, then newly discovered at Pompeii and Herculaneum.

ROMANTICISM Summed up by the poet Goethe in his phrase "feeling is everything," the Romantic movement dominated the 19th century. It was inspired

by both social revolution and a need for relief from Classical restraint.

PROGRAM MUSIC This term refers to music composed with a specific inspiration, reflected in its title and construction. Beethoven's *Pastoral Symphony* is program music.

IMPRESSIONISM A late 19th century style that develops the concept of program music by representing the pure atmosphere or mood of a theme rather than any literal or narrative aspect, as in Debussy's *La Mer*.

SERIALISM A revolutionary 12-note system of composition developed by Arnold Schoenberg to bridge the gap between conventional tonal music and the undisciplined atonal form.

Index

Acknowledgments

The publisher would like to thank:
Horniman Museum, London, also Dr. Frances Palmer and the staff of the Musicology Department for their assistance. Pitt Rivers Museum, University of Oxford, also Dr. Hélène La Rue and the staff of the Ethnomusicology Department for their assistance. Phelps Ltd, London, also Rachel Doublas and Gerry Mckensie for their assistance. Hill, Norman and Beard Ltd, Thaxted, also Andrew Rae and Richard Webb for their assistance. Bill Lewington Ltd, London; Boosey and Hawkes Ltd, London; Empire Drums and Percussion Ltd, London; Simmons Electric Percussion Ltd, London; Vintage and Rare Guitars Ltd, London John Clark; Adam Glasser; Malcolm Healey; Chris Cross; John Walters for the loan of equipment

and assistance. Janice Lacock for extensive editorial work on the early stages of the book. Tim Hammond for editorial assistance. Lynn Bresler for the index.
Jonathan Buckley for his help on the photographic sessions.
Tetra Designs for making the models photographed on pp.6-7.

Picture credits
t=top b=bottom m=middle l=left r=right
J. Allan Cash Ltd: 19t, 24m, 50r, 51l, 56b
E.T. Archives: 8tl
Barnaby's Picture Library: 13br, 17tr
Bridgeman Art Library: 12tl, 16b, 21lm, 26b, 29r, 30t, 30m, 35tr, 36tr, 38t, 40m, 50b
British Library: 70-71
Corbis: 64cl; Archivo Iconografico, S.A 66tr, 66br; Dave Bartruff 64bc; Bettmann 65cr,

65ac, 66bl; Christopher Cormack 67tl; Shelley Gazin 68tr; Angelo Hornak 69c; Hulton-Deutsch Collection 65bc; Bill Ross 69b; S.I.N. 70cr; Arthur Thevenart 65tl
Joe Cornish: 64crb
Doublas Dickens: 55m
Mary Evans Picture Library: 6r, 10tl, 11tr, 11m, 15tr, 18m, 19b, 20tr, 22tl, 24b, 26t, 29t, 34tr, 36tl, 37b, 38l, 46m, 46b, 50tl, 4m, 57m
Fine Art Photographic Library Ltd: 5mr, 22tr, 36bl, 42t
John R. Freeman: 29b
Sonia Halliday Photographs: 18t, 36b
Robert Harding Library: 6bl, 39t, 41t; Roger Markham-Smith, International Stock 68cr
Michael Holford: 8tr, 28tl, 36m, 37m
Hutchinson Library, 42r, 38m

Image Bank: 6tr, 53t
Junior Department Royal College of Music: 71cr
London Features International Ltd: 49r, 61tl, 62
Mansell Collection: 16tl, 17m, 20b, 21rm, 24t, 30l
John Massey Stewart: 28mr, 37tr
National Gallery: 44l
David Redfern: 14m, 13br, 22l
Singapore Symphony Orchestra: 66-67
Stone / Getty Images: Andy Sacks 69tc
Thames and Hudson Ltd: 46t
Topexpress: 48bl
Picture research by Millie Trowbridge.
Illustrations by Coral Mula, Will Giles and Sandra Pond.
Jacket images: James Noble/Corbis, b.
All other images © Dorling Kindersley.
For more information see: www.dkimages.com